Enid Byford has had several career: trained upon leaving school), as a te school, as a freelance writer/photograpner in Singapore and Canada, and most recently as an editor – the last ten of her seventeen years in Ottawa were as managing editor of Canadian Geographic. Since returning with her husband to Somerset at the beginning of 1984 she has worked as freelance editor/proof reader. Last year, with Eileen Holloway, she produced a *A Somerset Sampler,* which led to the writing of *Somerset Curiosities.*

Frontispiece: Taunton Castle, the leather reproduction of the tower of St Mary Magdalene (see No. 48).

Somerset Curiosities

Enid Byford

THE DOVECOTE PRESS

Somerset Curiosities

First published in 1987 by The Dovecote Press Ltd
Stanbridge, Wimborne, Dorset BH21 4JD

ISBN 0 946159 48 3

Photoset in Palatino by Character Graphics
Taunton, Somerset
Printed and bound by Biddles Ltd
Guildford and King's Lynn

5 7 9 8 6 4

Contents

Somerset Curiosities

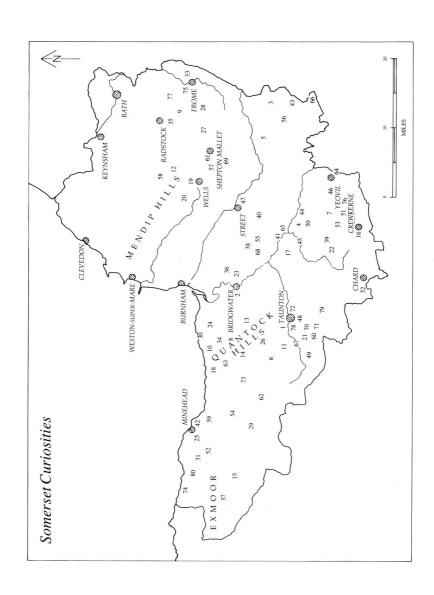

N

MILES

0   10   20

CLEVEDON

WESTON-SUPER-MARE

BURNHAM

MINEHEAD

E X M O O R

KEYNSHAM

BATH

M E N D I P   H I L L S

RADSTOCK

FROME

WELLS

SHEPTON MALLET

STREET

QUANTOCK HILLS

BRIDGWATER

TAUNTON

CHARD

YEOVIL

CREWKERNE

74
80
37
15
31
52
25 42
59
29
54
62
73
18 10 34
63
14 78
2
36 23
30 24
13
1
78 72
48
67 21 70
49 60 71
6
11
79
26
38 55
68
41 65
17
45 4
22 39
50
44
7
53 51 76
46
64
16
32
5
40
47
3
56
43
66
20 19
57 61
27
69
58 12
35
9 75 33
77
28

Acknowledgements

Many people have helped with the compilation of this book, too many to name individually, but I must thank four: David Bromwich of the Local History Library for his patient and generous help in locating the material that added an extra touch to the story; Marie Siraut, Assistant Editor of the Victoria History of Somerset, for her part in preparing the manuscript; Robert Dunning, Editor of the Victoria History, who not only corrected errors of history but also pointed out editorial lapses; and lastly, my husband, who, in this his eightieth year, took over the kitchen and made it easier to meet a tight publication deadline.

I am also grateful to the following for their help in providing the illustrations: Colin Byford (for the drawings), Julian Comrie, Somerset County Museum, courtesy Peter Birch, Taunton Deane Borough Council, Admiral Blake Museum, Street Shoe Museum, and Douglas Allen Photography, Bridgwater.

1 One Of The Gems Of The Great Exhibition

Position: In Somerset County Museum, Taunton Castle
Ordnance Map: Taunton and Lyme Regis; Sheet 193 1:50 000
Map Ref: ST 2230/2455
Access: Taunton Castle is in the centre of the town and can be reached from North Street through the gateway beside the SWEB showrooms, or from Corporation Street. There is a car park within the castle grounds for visitors to the museum.

Note: A craftsman named John Steevens of Taunton, who set up as a 'complete house furnisher' in 1836, carved a magnificent cabinet for the 1851 Great Exhibition. A contemporary note states that 'The Cabinet by Mr Stevens [sic] of Taunton has attracted much attention in the Crystal Palace as well for the taste of its execution as for the beauty of the wood of which it is composed and the richness of its general effect. It is a sumptuous and elegant work and one which does much to uphold the credit of British furniture manufacturers. Certainly in the article of furniture we cannot but congratulate our native workmen on the ability they have shown and the excellent manner in which they have asserted their true position among the manufacturers of the world.' The Commissioner of the United States offered free transport for the cabinet to the US International Exhibition, but Mr Steevens preferred to make a sale in Britain. The grandfather of Mrs Mary Fillis Gibson bought the cabinet for his home at Roscraddoc Manor in Cornwall, and there it remained until 1963 when Mrs Gibson bequeathed it to the County of Somerset. It is a superb example of Victorian craftsmanship, although the majority of housewives today would probably shudder at the thought of keeping the intricate carvings clean!

Places of interest in the Neighbourhood
48. The Tower That's Made Of Leather (Taunton)
72. Where Lepers Once Were Tended (Taunton)
78. The Toads That Children Love (Taunton)

Food and Accommodation
Ample available in Taunton

2 The Riot Trial Salver

Position. Bridgwater
Ordnance Map. Weston-super-Mare & Bridgwater area; Sheet 182 1:50 000
Map Ref. ST 3000/3700
Access. In the Admiral Blake Museum, Blake Street

Note. A General Election was held in 1832 and there were in Bridgwater a number of electors who felt that the owner of *The Alfred, London Weekly Journal*, and *Bridgwater and Somersetshire General Advertiser* (established in 1831 so that John Bown might express his views freely) was unduly biased in his editorials before the electon. Despite the fact that his candidates (Tories) were not elected several dissidents went to the editor's home, broke in, and helped themselves to the contents of his cellar. Mr Bowen was sent for and, while trying to disperse the rob, was badly beaten up and left insensible. A fracas ensued, leading to the Riot Act being read and a number of Bridgwater citizens being arrested.

For some reason, five were tried at Taunton and acquitted on a technicality; the remainder were taken to Wells for trial and the proceedings lasted longer than had been expected. The defendants and members of the jury were all housed for the night at the same lodgings. That night everyone got together (even to the extent of sharing the same beds), a considerable amount of alcohol was imbibed. Next morning in court, despite incontrovertible evident to the contrary, the jury found all the defendants not guilty and they were released. Someone must have suggested that it would be appropriate to show their gratitude to the defending counsel because a salver containing some 26 ounces of silver was purchased and suitably inscribed:

PRESENTED
TO
BENJAMIN LOVIBOND ESQ
for his Generous and Independent Conduct in
Gratuitously and Successfully
DEFENDING
at the Somerset Spring Assizes and Quarter Sessions of 1833
THIRTY EIGHT PERSONS
WHO WERE UNJUSTLY ACCUSED OF
Conspiracy and Riot
during the Election of Members for the
Borough of Bridgwater
in December 1832

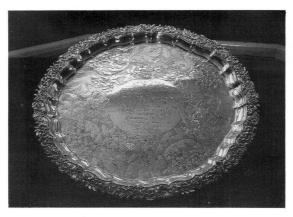

The salver needs to be seen; the engraver really went to town using every style of lettering in his manual (a very fine silversmith was obviously responsible for the crafting of the salver itself). Not long ago, the administrator of the museum learned that the salver was available for sale in the Channel Islands. The museum has no funds (it is run by voluntary staff); but when the borough was abolished in the local government reorganisation trustees were oppointed to administer its former funds and property. The trustees wre approached and the salver was brought back to Bridgwater. It is the more interesting because Jarman's *History of Bridgwater* (published 1889) credits one Mr Serjeant Kinglake with defending 37 persons – the salver tells a different tale.

As you go out of the museum, glance up and see whether there is a flag over the building – if so, it will be the Commonwealth Jack, and unlikely to be seen anywhere else in Britain, as it was flown only between 1649 and 1658. It reflects the break with Scotland at that time, having on the vertical side nearest the hoist (the part nearest the flagpole) the Cross of St George – sideways on to its position on our present flag – and on the part known as the fly (that farthest from the mast) the gold irish harp on a blue ground. Scotland rejoined the Union in 1654, but not until April 1658 did the St Andrew's Cross appear again on the flag, when the Irish harp was placed on a shield in the centre; with the restoration of the monarchy in 1660 back came the Union Jack.

Places of interest in the Neighbourhood
  8. Site Of A Victorian Scandal (Four Forks)
 13. Home Of The Original Of Frankenstein (Brookfield)
 23. The Never Open Gate (Chedzoy)
 36. Site Of The Last Battle In England (Westonzoyland)

Food and Accommodation
Plenty available in Bridgwater

3 The Man Who Built His Own Monument

Position: In the Churchyard of St Peter & St Paul Church, Wincanton
Ordnance Map: Yeovil to Frome; Sheet 183 1:50 000
Map Ref: ST 7145/2855
Access: Follow the one-way system through the town until you see the church on your right: there is a free car-park just beyond on the same side of the road.

Note: Nathaniel Ireson was pleased with himself, and justifiably so. He was not well educated, but in his time he had been an architect, a brick maker, builder, designer, sculptor, plasterer, skilled potter, church warden, as well as being a land-, house- and quarry-owner. Ireson was born in 1686, probably at Ansley near Nuneaton, but by 1711 he was living in Wiltshire. Between 1720 and 1722 he built, to Colin Campbell's design, Stourhead for Henry Hoare. About 1726 Ireson had become properous enough to buy Windmill Farm near Wincanton. This farm proved to be a very sound investment. It had a bed of very good workable building stone, sand, and clay suitable for his brick-making enterprise as well as another kind of clay that was suitable for the pottery he established at Wincanton. Incidentally, Ireson's pottery pieces, especially the dated ones, are much sought after by collectors.

Not long after buying the farm he pulled down the existing dwelling and built Ireson House (where he lived until his death in April 1769). He continued to build and alter several houses in Wincanton, including The Dogs, which had gained fame for sheltering William of Orange for one night when he was on his way to London in 1688.

Nathaniel Ireson was a devout churchman; in 1748 he built, at his own expense, the chancel of Wincanton Church (it was replaced when the entire church was rebuilt in the 1880s). Several memorial tablets in that church were carved by him, and there are others in several Wiltshire churches. He also built Redlynch Chapel and the chancel of Bruton Church. The statue in Wincanton churchyard is stated to have been carved by Nathaniel himself; the pedestal on which it now stands is a replacement, and later members of the family are also recorded on it.

Places of interest in the Neighbourhood
  5. The Gaol Built With Funds Filched From The Poor (Castle Cary)
 43. The Panel That Toppled A Religious Order (Templecombe)
 56. Road Taxes Of The Past (South Cheriton)

Food and Accommodation
Ample available in Wincanton

14

4 The Two Little Brothers Who Never Were Parted

Position: On the north side of the Petherton Bridge on the A303
Ordnance Map: Taunton and Lyme Regis; Sheet 193 1:50 000
Map Ref: ST 4501/1675

Note: The two worn stone figures on the side of Petherton Bridge
(hidden all too often amid nettles and other vegetation in the summer)
are now a National Monument. One story has it that they commemorate
two children who drowned in the River Parrett many years ago. The
legend is that their parents had been childless for some twenty years and
when, eventually, twin sons were born, the couple could not bear to let
them out of their sight. The children were forbidden to go anywhere
without one or other parent being with them. Then, one day, the father
and mother had to go to Yeovil for some urgent shopping. The boys
slipped out of the house and went to play by the river. One fell in and,
although neither had learnt to swim, the other went into the water to try
and rescue his brother. Both drowned, and two days later, on what
would have been their twelfth birthday, the bodies were found still
clasping each other.

The other story is not nearly so sentimental; it is that one figure is
female and both are adults – the couple who first paid for the bridge to be
built in the 15th century – but as nothing more seems to be known of
them, and as imagination is needed when looking at the figures, you are
free to choose which story you prefer.

If you continue along the A303, you will be driving along part of the
route of the Foss(e) Way, the military road built by the Romans in the
middle of the 1st century AD to link Axmouth with Lincoln. The Roman
roads were as straight as possible (the Foss Way deviated less than six
miles over its 200 mile length), and today several of our older arterial
roads follow the same route laid down by the Romans.

Places of interest in the Neighbourhood
22. This Clock Has Ten Faces – And Still Is Inaccurate (Barrington)
39. A Painted Chimneypiece (Barrington)
44. Where A Saxon George Fights His Dragon (Stoke-sub-Hamdon)
50. The Painted Doors Of St Mary's Church (Norton-sub-Hamdon)

Food and Accommodation
Food available at nearby Stoke-sub-Hamdon and South Petherton;
accommodation in local farmhouses and at Yeovil

15

5 The Gaol Built With Funds Filched From the Poor

Position: On Bailey Hill in the centre of Castle Cary
Ordnance Map: Yeovil to Frome; Sheet 183 1:50 000
Map Ref: ST 6390/3245

Note: David Luellyn (or Llewellin) a 'chirurgion', sometime before his death in 1605, 'gave unto the poore of this parish tenn poundes to remayne in stock to their use for ever and to be ordered yearly by the Churchwardens and Overseers of the poore for the tyme beinge', and John Francis, about the same time, left 'the interest of £2 to this Church for ever and the interest of tenpounds to the poor at Easter for ever' – the poor in both cases being residents of Castle Cary. For more than 170 years the trustees distributed the income as instructed at Eastertide. Then, in 1779, the administrators voted that the money should be used instead to build a lock-up for offenders. On the stone building a notice states: 'This Round House (one of only four in the county) was built in 1779 by Mr W. M. Clark for £23 (from Local Charities) as a temporary prison or lock-up. It is 7ft in diameter and 10ft high with two iron grills for ventilation. In 1894 it was repaired as a result of 1/- subscription, and in 1922 the Lord of the Manor, Sir Henry Hoare, Bart., J. P., presented it to the Parish Council.'

The gaol usually housed drunks overnight, but on March 3, 1785, the third resolution passed by the Early Sunday School Committee reads: 'That after the schools are commenced, if any children above the age of seven years are found in the streets etc., breaking the sabbath, they shall be taken and locked up in the Round House during school hours.' Well, that was one way of ensuring that parents had a quiet Sunday afternoon!

Places of interest in the Neighbourhood
3. The Man Who Built His Own Monument (Wincanton)
56. Road Taxes Of The Past (South Cheriton)

Food and Accommodation
Both are available in Castle Cary

6 Is The Font Inverted?

Position: In Lydeard St Lawrence Church
Ordnance Map: Minehead and Brendon Hills; Sheet 181 1:50 000
Map Ref: ST 3215/1275

Note: When Charles I was tried in Westminster Hall, of the 135 Commissioners nominated by the Commons to be judges and jury only 62 turned up, among them John Venn, a native of Lydeard St Lawrence. He had been one of the six members of Parliament who, together with those charged with treason, had been excepted from the King's Pardon on June 17, 1642 because he had fomented a gathering of citizens protesting conditions in the country the previous December. When the Civil War began, Venn, a former captain sergeant major in the Artillery Company, became a colonel of foot in the Parliamentary Army. He fought at Worcester in September 1642 and became the Governor of Windsor Castle in October, remaining in that position until 1645. During his custodianship, Venn plundered St George's Chapel and destroyed the furniture and decorations. His name appears among the fifty-nine signatories to the warrant that sentenced Charles I to be beheaded on January 30, 1649. Eleven years later, upon the restoration of Charles II, the regicides themselves were put on trial, but by then John Venn had gone before a higher judge, having died peacefully at his home on June 28, 1658 at the age of 64.

Some say the people of Lydeard St Lawrence were so angry with John Venn for his part in the execution that they upended the font so that their children should not be christened in the same basin as a regicide. Historians believe this is an unlikely story, that during restoration work the original top was damaged and it was decided to carve a new basin from the solid stone at the base.

Places of interest in the Neighbourhood
   8. Site Of A Victorian Scandal (Four Forks)
  11. The Mysterious Monument (Heathfield)
  13. Home Of The Original Of Frankenstein (Broomfield)
  26. The 'Lady Shrine' That Is No Lady (West Bagborough)

Food and Accommodation
Good food obtainable at The Lethbridge Arms and at The Bell at Bishops Lydeard also at the Farmers Arms just off the A358 at Combe Florey. Ample accommodation in Taunton.

7 Tom Coryate's Much Travelled Shoes

Position: Church of St Peter and St Paul, Odcombe
Ordnance Map: Yeovil to Frome; Sheet 183 1:50 000
Map Ref: ST 5065/1545

Note: Tom, son of George Coryate, the rector of Odcombe, was a droll young man, and after leaving university in 1596 and fooling around for a few years, he managed to become a sort of court comic to James I following the death of Elizabeth. Prince Henry, son of James, took a liking to Tom and when he set up his own establishment, Tom went with him. George Coryate died, probably in 1607 and he probably left Tom some money, because in May 1608, Tom set off from Dover for France and five months of travelling. He travelled light – according to his report he took only one extra shirt and wore the same shoes throughout his journeyings through France, what is now Italy, Switzerland and along the Rhine. By the time he returned to England in October, he reckoned he had covered 1,975 miles, mainly on foot. At one time he was threatened by thieves, whereupon Tom threw his hat down on the ground and began to beg for alms – which the thieves gave him. When he returned, Tom wrote a book, *Coryats Crudities*, detailing his travels. It was the first guidebook ever for travellers to Europe, and Tom found it difficult to find a publisher. He hit upon the idea of approaching well known people and asking them to write an introduction (in rhyme) to his book. Eventually he persuaded 66 celebrities to introduce his book and Ben Jonson then edited the verses that ran to 108 out of the more than 800 pages of the finished work. Prince Henry then added his influence and a bookseller was found in 1611 to publish the book, which sold well. Today, only two perfect copies are known to exist (one is in the Chetham Library, the other in Taunton's Local History Library), but if you have an engraving from Tom's *Crudities*, treasure it well, it is valuable.

By 1612, Tom's feet were itching to travel again. Before taking off for a ten-year trip to the Middle East and India, he hung up his much travelled shoes in Odcombe church where they became objects of much interest for well over a hundred years. Tom didn't return from his epic journeying – he died of dysentery in Surat in December 1617, at about 40 years of age. Apart from his guidebook, which remained the only one for many years, Tom is credited with the introduction, from Italy, of table forks.

Places of interest in the Neighbourhood
4. The Two Little Brothers Who Never Were Parted (Petherton)
51. The Carpet On Which Once Stood A Throne (West Coker)
76. The Carving By A Hero's Widow (West Coker)

Food and Accommodation
Available in Montacute and West Coker

The remains of the Chapel of the community at Agapemone.

8 Site Of A Victorian Scandal

Position: Agapemone, Four Forks near Spaxton
Ordnance Map: Weston-super-Mare & Bridgwater area, Sheet 182
1:500 000
Map Ref: ST 2330/3695
Access: Agapemone is on the same side of the road as the Lamb Inn
(which is just beyond it) on the road from Four Forks to Barford House

Note: Victorians were deliciously scandalised by the goings on at
Spaxton – or what they imagined was going on at Spaxton. It started
during the 1846 annual holiday of the parish priest of nearby Charlynch,
the Rev Mr Samuel Starky. His curate, the Rev Henry James Prince
announced to a startled congregation that he was the embodiment of the
Second Coming of the Messiah and that from henceforth marriage
should be a spiritual affair. So persuasive were his arguments that he
soon collected around him several adherents, including his own parish
priest. Prince, known to his adoring flock as 'Beloved', had, before
going to Charlynch, married an elderly spinster and, upon her death,
inherited a hefty fortune (which her indignant relatives tried
unsuccessfully to recover for themselves).

The widowed Beloved then married Julia Starky, the sister of his
former parish priest and they moved to Suffolk for a while and preached
and converted quite a number of folk, including the Nottidge sisters
from Clare in Suffolk. Five daughters each received £6,000 upon the
death of their father; three decided to go to Spaxton and join forces with
Prince. This windfall, plus the worldly goods of other converts, enabled
the community to buy land outside Spaxton and to build Agapemone,
the Abode of Love. Soon, hordes of workmen surrounded the estate with
a high wall in the middle of which was an 20-bedroomed house that also
contained several reception rooms. In the grounds were some cottages
and gazebos. Speculation ran riot as to what actually happened within
the walls. The villagers knew when 'Beloved' was in residence because
a flag bearing the symbol of a lamb then floated over the house; they also
knew (probably from the workmen), that the chapel was most peculiarly
furnished with a Turkish carpet, several armchairs and a couch covered
with blue velvet, as well as a billiards table. Apart from that they knew
little – outsiders were not admitted, but it was noted that the disciples
were quiet, strictly honest in fiscal matters and charitable in their
dealings.

21

Prince persuaded the Nottidge sisters to form spiritual marriages with three of his 'anointed ones'; a fourth sister was induced to go to Spaxton, but was soon rescued by her family. Then Agnes, one of the spiritual wives, became pregnant and was sent away. After that Beloved felt the need to have a truly spiritual wife in the form of a young virgin – she produced a child and this so upset the Rev Lewis Price and his wife, the former Harriet Nottidge, that they quit, taking her £6,000 with them; the remainder of the congregation are reported to have blamed the mother while Beloved went serenely on his way.

In 1899 he confounded his flock by dying, but in 1902, one John Hugh Smyth-Pigott discovered that the cloak of the Messiah had fallen upon his shoulders. He, too, had been a clergyman and he also was given to irregular behaviour in his unions. Despite having an attractive wife, he installed another lady as his Chief Soul Bride, and by her had three children. The Bishop of Bath & Wells unfrocked him in 1909. The community remained very withdrawn and managed to escape press attention after that until March 1927 when Smyth-Pigott died. Attention flared briefly in 1936 with the death and secret burial of Mrs Smyth-Pigott, and again in 1956 when the Chief Soul Bride, now leader of the aging community, Ruth Smyth, died. That was the only time that outsiders were admitted to the place of worship.

Agapemone was sold in 1958 to a developer who divided it into flats, and so, once more, the Abode of Love may be viewed only from the outside. However, if you go into The Lamb Inn there is a ground plan of Agapemone to show just how complex was the organisation.

Places of interest in the Neighbourhood
2. The Riot Trial Salver (Bridgwater)
13. Home Of The Original Of Frankenstein (Broomfield)
36. Site Of The Last Battle In England (Westonzoyland)

Food and accommodation
Plenty available in Bridgwater

9 The Horse In The Church

Position: In St Andrew's Church, Mells
Ordnance Map: Yeovil to Frome; Sheet 183 1:50 000
Map Ref: ST 7280/4925
Access: At the end of a cul-de-sac off the main street in Mells

Note: The first equestrian sculpture by Sir Alfred Munnings, the famous
painter of horses, was commissioned by the family of Edward Horner,
last male heir to the Horner estate during the First World War. He was
killed in 1917 at Cambrai and is shown in bronze, mounted on his horse.
The excellence of the moulding of the animal led to the Jockey Club
commissioning Munnings to make the statue of the racehorse, Brown
Jack, that is now at Epsom Racecourse. Edward's sister, Katherine,
married Raymond Asquith, son of the Liberal Prime Minister, and her
side of the family eventually inherited the Horner estates.

Buried in the churchyard are a number of well known people,
including Lady Violet Bonham Carter and Monsignor Ronald Knox, the
Roman Catholic theologian.

Places of interest in the Neighbourhood
28. Nunney's Moving Cross
75. The Mini-Follies Of Frome
77. The Church In The Farmyard (Hardington Bampfylde)

Food and Accommodation
Food available in Mells; hotel accommodation at Nunney

10 Where Somerset Was Going To Rival Texas

Position: Kilve
Ordnance Map: Minehead and Brendon Hills; Sheet 181 1:50 000
Map Ref: ST 1450/4430
Access: From the A39 at Kilve, turn north and follow the road towards the coast as far as it will go

Note: Alongside Kilve Pill, a creek used by smugglers during the Napoleonic Wars, stands a Grade II Historic Monument. It is a brick-built retort dating from the early 1920s, the most substantial relic of the days when geologists thought that Somerset might one day rival Texas in the production of oil. In 1916 it had been noted that the cliffs north of Kilve contained bituminous Liassic shales. An exploratory borehole entered the shales at 91m depth and was still among shales when boring ceased at 168m; exploration had shown, in fact, that the oil-bearing beds reached a depth of about 300m (1,000 ft) and covered some 8,000 acres, extending up to two miles inland. The report of one geologist was ecstatic, stating that 'Oil has had its romances in the past, equal to gold or diamonds, but nothing in those surpasses the discovery of oil shale in West Somerset for sheer human interest and potential National importance. A vast assemblage of black and white beds composes the cliffs which stretch from Watchet to Combwich. It may be safely stated that these beds are the thickest in the world. The new discovery places England at once in the front rank of cheap fuel-producing countries...' The Shalin Company was formed to exploit the find; the yield was found to be 156 litres of oil to the cubic metre of shale, and several hundred barrels of oil were recovered before the venture was abandoned in 1924 because the cost of production was far too high. Today the site is overgrown and visitors picnic and walk along the cliff paths overlooking the sea. The retort is now a picturesque ruin.

As you drive along Sea Lane to the site, on your left you will see a ruined building attached to an old farmhouse. This was known as Kilve Priory, although its only known ecclesiastical connection was from 1329 to about the end of that century when it was a residence for a college of priests. It then became part of the farm. During the Napoleonic Wars and later, smugglers found it a useful place to store their contraband until one night, when the customs men were too close for comfort, a smuggler set fire to a brandy barrel to destroy the evidence, also causing the 'priory' to blow up and be partially destroyed.

Places of interest in the Neighbourhood
18. The Village Where Time Seems To Stand Still (East Quantoxhead)
30. The Port That Was (Lilstock)
34. The Dog Pound (And Why It Was Built) (Holford)

Food and Accommodation
Some good restaurants on the A39 westwards, and several bed and breakfast establishments as well as hotels, otherwise make for Minehead

11 The Mysterious Monument

Position: St John the Baptist Church, Heathfield
Ordnance Map: Taunton and Lyme Regis; Sheet 193 1:50 000
Map Ref: ST 1595/2650

Note: Two kneeling figures facing each other across a faldstool are on
the north side of the chancel in Heathfield parish church. The beautifully
preserved figures of a bare-headed man in a black doublet and a lady
wearing a pleated petticoat, tight fitting bodice and the long-veiled Paris
head-dress of the late 16th century, are a delight to behold, but no one
knows exactly who is commemorated. The most probable candidates are

Margaret Hadley, the heiress to the manors of Heathfield and Withycombe, and her brother Arthur. Arthur died in 1558 by which time Margaret had already married Thomas Luttrell of Dunster and had taken the manors to that family. After Thomas died, Margaret married John Strode of Parnham, and then following John's death, she married Richard Hill. Thomas was commemorated at Dunster and John at Parnham, and so the candidates for the male figure are Richard or Arthur. Authorities suggest that as Margaret and Arthur were close as children and worshipped at Heathfield, the memorial was raised by Margaret to Arthur and herself during her lifetime. The Latin inscription is painted on a board and is no longer decipherable. See also the entry for East Quantoxhead (18) concerning Margaret's marriage to Thomas Luttrell.

Places of interest in the Neighbourhood
  1. One Of The Gems Of The Great Exhibition (Taunton)
 67. Where's Chilly Green? (Oake)
 70. The Grand Canal That Wasn't So Grand (Nynehead)
 72. Where Lepers Once Were Tended (Taunton)
 78. The Toads That Children Love (Taunton)

Food and Accommodation
Plenty available in Taunton

12 The Italian Monument In An English Field

Position: West Horrington
Ordnance Map: Weston-super-Mare & Bridgwater area; Sheet 182
1:50 000
Map Ref: ST 5705/4890
Access: In a field on the east side of the Bath-Wells A39, opposite the
TV mast on Pen Hill

Note: During the 1939-45 War a number of Italian prisoners were
employed in agriculture on Somerset farms. Several German bombs fell
one night on land belonging to Mr Wellstead-White, badly damaging the
boundary wall. Castrano Celestra, an Italian stonemason, was sent to
rebuild the wall and he received permission to put up a monument (in his
spare time) as a thank offering to the local people who had treated the
Italian prisoners of war so well. The monument, which probably was
larger than Mr Wellstead-White expected, stands 12ft high on four scaly
pillars and represents the Roman statue of the twin boys, Romulus and
Remus, being suckled by their wolf foster mother. Legend has it that
their mother was a vestal virgin named Rhea Sylvia and their father was
Mars. Their uncle Amulius ordered them to be drowned at birth together
with their mother. The twins were miraculously saved and reared by the
she-wolf. Later, in 753 BC, while the young men were building the city
that became Rome, Romulus killed Remus for laughing at his walls on
the Palatine. Romulus later provided wives for his citizens by the 'rape
of the Sabines', a far cry from Mr Wellstead-White's field in Somerset
(thank heavens).

Places of interest in the Neighbourhood
19. The Ceiling They Didn't Know Was There (Wells)
20. The Waxworks That Thrilled The Georgians (Wookey Hole)
58. The Stained Glass Found In A Ditch (Chewton Mendip)

Food and Accommodation
Plenty of both available at Wells

13 Home Of The Original Of Frankenstein

Position: Broomfield
Ordnance Map: Weston-super-Mare & Bridgwater area; Sheet 182
1:50 000
Map Ref: ST 2225/3210
Access: After reaching the village of Broomfield, follow the National
Trust for Nature Conservation signs to Fyne Court.

Note: Andrew Crosse, owner of Fyne Court in the early 19th century,
was a local magistrate, wealthy landowner and a pioneer of electricity.
He was known locally as the Wizard of Broomfield and once claimed
that insects had appeared in his voltaic battery experiments. The rector
of Broomfield, a cleric named Smith, denounced Mr Crosse from the
pulpit for practising the black arts, and other residents in the village
accused him of causing storms by his atmospheric electricity
experiments. One of the masts he erected for those experiments may still
be seen among the trees today. Mary Shelley, wife of the poet, heard of
the activities and accusations against Andrew Crosse and the stories
inspired her to write *Frankenstein or the Modern Prometheus*, published
in 1818. Scientists and other thinkers of the period thought highly of
Andrew Crosse and many came to visit him, including Sir Humphrey
Davy and Sidney Smith. That Crosse was no mere dabbler in his
experimentation may be judged by the fact that he spent about £3,000
annually on scientific apparatus, but alas, little remains on record today
of his work. In 1894 a fire swept through the house destroying not only
most of the building, but all of Crosse's scientific records stored there.
The stables and music room of Andrew Crosse's house survived, and
today the Somerset Trust for Nature Conservation has its headquarters
there, leasing the property from The National Trust, which acquired
Fyne Court for the nation in 1972.

Places of interest in the Neighbourhood
2. The Riot Trial Salver (Bridgwater)
6. Is The Font Inverted? (Lydeard St Lawrence)
8. Site Of A Victorian Scandal (Four Forks)

Food and Accommodation
Ample available in Bridgwater

14 The Hill Surveyed By Schoolboys

Position: Wills Neck, Quantock Hills
Ordnance Map: Minehead and Brendon Hills; Sheet 181 1:50 000
Map Ref: ST 1650/3515
Access: Take the Cothelstone/Bridgwater road out of Bishops Lydeard;
turn left at the top of the hill beyond Cothelstone at the West Bagborough
signpost and continue up the hill, following the road marked 'Car Park'.
Follow the map (on foot) from the top of Lydeard Hill to Wills Neck.

Note: William Cornish Badcock, a native of West Somerset (the name
Badcock appears frequently among the memorials in Kilve parish
church), was a teacher of physics at Bristol's Clifton College from 1922
to 1945, and a keen walker. His enthusiasm for walking led him to take
parties of schoolboys for outings to the Quantock Hills, and his expertise
led him to demonstrate the practicalities of his subject by showing the
boys how to survey terrain. Wills Neck contains the highest point in the
Quantocks (384m), and 'Bertie' Badcock's students, having established
the position of that point, gradually made a cairn there by the means of
each boy adding a stone on each outing to the spot. When eventually the
official survey was made, the triangulation pillar was set exactly in the
centre of the schoolboys' cairn.

Places of interest in the Neighbourhood
  6. Is The Font Inverted? (Lydeard St Lawrence)
 26. The 'Lady Shrine' That Is No Lady (West Bagborough)

Food and Accommodation
Good food available at The Lethbridge Arms and The Bell at Bishops
Lydeard. Plenty of bed and breakfast accommodation at farms in area,
but for hotel accommodation, go to Taunton.

15 The Village Where Eight Bridges Aren't Enough

Position: Winsford
Ordnance Map: Minehead and Brendon Hills; Sheet 181 1:50 000
Map Ref: ST 9070/3500

Note: Winsford is a picturesque little village situated where four roads meet at the confluence of the River Exe and Winn Brook. As a result, the village seems to have an excess of bridges. At least three stone bridges carry traffic; another one is cobbled and is the original packhorse bridge; there are three wooden foot bridges and, according to the large-scale map, another two away from the centre of the village. You would think that with so many means of crossing water, everyone and everything could pass over in dryness – not so – the road leading to the church has no bridge and so one fords the Exe at that point.

Opposite the Wesleyan chapel is the cottage where was born Ernest Bevin, the Minister of Labour and National Service in the 1939-45 War and Foreign Secretary in Attlee's post-War government. Also associated with Winsford was R. D. Blackmore, who wrote part of *Lorna Doone* while staying at the Royal Oak Inn, the attractive thatched building that faces the packhorse bridge (now a National Monument).

Places of interest in the Neighbourhood
31. The Stone Beehive (Allerford)
37. The Case Of The Missing Body (Cow Castle)
52. The Oldest Dovecote In England? (Blackford)
80. The Steepest Motorable Hill In England (Porlock)

Food and Accommodation
There are two or three restaurants and good hotels in Winsford. Exford and Dulverton also have hotels and restaurants.

16 The Brass That Became A Soap Advert

Position: St Bartholomew's Church, Crewkerne
Ordnance Map: Taunton and Lyme Regis; Sheet 193 1:50 000
Map Ref: ST 4395/0975

Note: On the west wall of the South Transept of the parish church at Crewkerne is a brass bearing the coat of arms of Adam Martin who died on December 20, 1678. The crest (only about 2 inches high) shows a monkey (or ape), with a collar around his neck and a chain around his waist, sitting on a tree stump and peering at his face in a hand mirror. Somehow, a publicity tycoon of the 1890s hit on the idea of using the Martin crest as an advertisement and so, well into this century, it appeared among the enamelled advertisements on railway stations and in newspapers as a reminder to housewives to buy Monkey Brand soap. This was not a 'soap' in the sense it could be used to wash with, but was a forerunner of scouring powders and was an essential item in almost every British household.

Places of interest in the Neighbourhood
 7. Tom Coryate's Much Travelled Shoes (Odcombe)
32. Printed In Germany (Chard)
51. The Carpet On Which Once Stood A Throne (West Coker)
76. The Carving By A Hero's Widow (West Coker)

Food and Accommodation
Several good pubs in Crewkerne; the Haselbury Inn at Haselbury Plucknett has very good food (but you may need to book ahead of time). Hotel accommodation in Crewkerne and at West Coker.

Winsford (see opposite).

17 The Tower Built By A Prime Minister

Position: Burton Pynsent
Ordnance Map: Taunton and Lyme Regis; Sheet 193 1:50 000
Map Ref: ST 3765/2420
Access: Take the Heale/Oath road north off the A378 at the west end of Curry Rivel. A public footpath leads to the Burton Pynsent Monument on the left.

Note: The monument, variously known as the Parkfield Monument, the Burton Steeple, and as Pynsent Tower, is a 150-ft-high column built on a cliff to overlook the lowlands of West Sedgemoor. Capability Brown, the landscape architect, submitted a design for a monument to William Pitt the Elder, but the top was probably made to Pitt's own idea. Apparently, when the government slapped 10/- tax on each hogshead of cider, Pitt had vigorously opposed it. Sir William Pynsent was the owner of estates at Burton that were affected by the levy; he had no legitimate children to whom to leave those estates and so he remade his will, naming Pitt as his heir, in gratitude for Pitt's opposition to the tax. Sir William died in 1765 and the monument was built at a cost of £2,000 in 1767. Now some £100,000 is needed for repairs to the tower.

There is a story that three times a cow wandered up the tower and twice was coaxed safely back to terra firma, but on the third occasion she suffered vertigo and crashed to her death from the viewing platform at the top. The field in which the tower stands is a favourite picnic spot, overlooking the Somerset levels, but until sufficient money has been raised to pay for repairs, the tower itself will have to remain closed.

Places of interest in the Neighbourhood
41. The Chapel Above The Road (Langport)
45. The Barrel Organ And The Buxom Angels (Muchelney)
65. When Langport Had Trains (And Floods) (Langport)

Food and Accommodation
There are several pubs in the area and good food is available at Langport, but hotel accommodation is limited and you will probably be better to make for Taunton or Yeovil if you haven't booked in advance.

18 The Village Where Time Seems to Stand Still

Position: East Quantoxhead
Ordnance Map: Minehead and Brendon Hills; Sheet 181 1:50 000
Map Ref: ST 1365/4360

Note: East Quantoxhead is a village that appears to have become set in time – a village pond is home to a number of ducks; all the cottages have obviously been there for at least 200 years, and the Court House outbuildings, which face onto the car park, are obviously of ancient origin. Court House itself is not open to the public, but the church is and so is the footpath that leads to the rocky cliffs overlooking Bridgwater Bay, some ½ mile away. It is easy to imagine, as you wander around the village, how it must have looked in earlier times. For once, the 20th century is not evident. The church contains an interesting sequel to the story of the Mysterious Monument (11), for here, according to a framed note in the church, Margaret Hadley, heiress to the manors of Heathfield and Withycombe, married her first husband, Thomas Luttrell, for the second time.

Margaret had been betrothed to her second cousin Thomas while still an infant, and her godmother was Thomas's mother, Dame Margaret Luttrell. In the eyes of the Roman Catholic church that made them spiritual brother and sister, and the cousinship was a further impediment to marriage. Thomas Luttrell and Margaret Hadley are thought to have been married privately during the reign of Edward VI, for during the reign of Mary they were sentenced to be divorced and excommunicated. They appealed to Pope Paul IV and were released from excommunication on condition that they 'made a new marriage in the face of the church'. By then Mary was dead and Elizabeth was on the throne. In 1560, ignoring the proceedings with Rome and the previous contract, Margaret, using her maiden name, was married to Thomas Luttrell in East Quantoxhead church. That was probably the last time that a remarriage of two persons divorced on the grounds of spiritual relationship took place in this country. One month after their remarriage, Margaret gave birth to a son, who eventually inherited Dunster Castle. Thomas died in 1571 and their marriage obviously had caused enough controversy for it to be stated on his tomb in Dunster Church 'being lawfully married unto Margaret Hadley'.

Places of interest in the Neighbourhood

Food and Accommodation

Food available at cafes and inns along the A39; accommodation at Minehead

19 The Ceiling They Didn't Know Was There

Position: In St Cuthbert's Church, Wells
Ordnance Map: Weston-super-Mare & Bridgwater area; Sheet 182
1:50 000
Map Ref: ST 5465/4570

Note: During repair work in the 1960s, workmen found that above the plastered ceiling of the side chapel in St Cuthbert's Church was a carved and panelled ceiling dating from the 15th century. The discovery of the traceried panels was quite a find as, over the years, many in other churches have disappeared during 'restoration' work; the plaster is thought to date from the late 18th or early 19th century.

Places of interest in the Neighbourhood
12. The Italian Monument In An English Field (West Horrington)
20. The Waxworks That Thrilled The Georgians (Wookey Hole)
47. Gracie Fields' First Clogs (Street)
58. The Stained Glass Found In A Ditch (Chewton Mendip)

Food and Accommodation
Both available in Wells

20 The Waxworks That Thrilled The Georgians

Position: Wookey Hole Caves
Ordnance Map: Weston-super-Mare & Bridgwater area;
Sheet 182 1:50 000
Map Ref: ST 5320/4795
Access: Follow signs to the caves

Note: Between 1802 and 1835, a Frenchwoman named Madame
Tussaud toured England with her wax models. She had been imprisoned
during the French Revolution and had begun her career modelling the
heads of guillotined aristocrats. During 1830 Mme Tussaud visited
Bath; recently archivists at the wax museum she founded in London
have helped the proprietors of the Wookey Hole Caves to set up a
Cabinet of Curiosities to re-create the Bath exhibits. Many of the wax
figures are cast from the original moulds and they include Louis XVI and
Queen Marie Antoinette, both of whom were modelled while Mme
Tussaud was a fellow prisoner in the Bastille.

Places of interest in the Neighbourhood
12. The Italian Monument In An English Field (West Horrington)
19. The Ceiling They Didn't Know Was There (Wells)

Food and Accommodation
Food available at Wookey Hole; accommodation in Wells

21 At The Sign Of The Footless Bird

Position: Langford Budville
Ordnance Map: Taunton and Lyme Regis; Sheet 193 1:50 000
Map Ref: ST 1105/2375
Access: The Martlet(t) Inn is on the main street in Langford Budville on the opposite side of the road to the church, and further into the village.

Note: A martlet is a heraldic symbol, based, it is believed, on the house martin and it is always shown without feet. Shown on a bearing or a crest, it indicates the fourth son of a family – usually someone who has no hope of inheriting money or property, and therefore no great catch for any lady. The pub is a pleasant inn dating back to the 17th century; it has an inglenook fireplace and a slate floor, and the food is worth making a lunchtime or evening visit for. There was obviously a slight mix-up over the spelling of the name as the inn sign shows one 't' and the painted name on the building gives two – the beer tastes just as well no matter how you spell the name.

Places of interest in the Neighbourhood
70. The Grand Canal That Wasn't So Grand (Nynehead)
71. The Changing Bells (Wellington)
79. Wellington's Monument (Wellington)

Food and Accommodation
Food is available at The Martlet; Taunton is within easy driving distance for accommodation

22 This Clock Has Ten Faces – And Still Is Inaccurate

Position: Barrington Court
Ordnance Map: Taunton and Lyme Regis; Sheet 193 1:50 000
Map Ref: ST 4000/1820

Note: On the lawns behind the main house at Barrington Court stands a splendid ten faced sundial (or facet-headed dial) made of stone and surmounted by a heraldic lion.

The earliest known sundial (dating from 340BC) was semicircular in shape, and was made by the Chaldean astronomer Berosus. The Romans, however, brought sundials to this country; later the Saxons used a form of sundial on church walls (scratch dial, or mass dial). These divided the day into four parts, possibly to indicate to the bell-ringer when he should toll the bell for the various services, but there was no attempt to obtain any accuracy in telling the time. Then an Arab mathematician in the 14th century took a more scientific approach and calculated how to construct and site sundials in order to obtain a degree of accuracy. Soon after that multiple dials began to appear, and the instrument at Barrington is an example of what is probably the most complex sundial. There is one problem with its timekeeping, it never can be accurate in this country. Colonel Lyle, who leased Barrington Court from The National Trust in the 1920s, bought one of a pair of sundials in California and shipped it to England. The dial was made in California and was calibrated for the latitude of that State, and so, no matter how it is sited in Somerset, it can only remain a curiosity.

Places of interest in the Neighbourhood
39. A Painted Chimneypiece (Barrington)
45. The Barrel Organ And The Buxom Angels (Muchelney)

Food and Accommodation
There are several pubs in Barrington and a number of bed-and-breakfast establishments in the vicinity, but for hotels and restaurants, go to Taunton, about 9 miles away.

23 The Never Open Gate

Position: Chedzoy Church
Ordnance Map: Weston-super-Mare & Bridgwater area; Sheet 182
1:50 000
Map Ref: ST 3405/3775
Access: The church is located on the Parchey/Sutton Mallet road, and
the gate is beyond, in the north west corner of the churchyard

Note: Tumble gates, also known as tumble-down stiles, were a means of
ensuring that animals could not gain access to an enclosed area. Seen
from a distance the gate appears to be a section of fence, but closer
examination shows that the post at one end is cut into V-shaped wedges
that fit one on top of the other and into each wedge fits one horizontal rail
of the fence. To go through the gate, push down on the ends of the rails
farthest away from the 'post' and step over. As soon as the end is
released, the wedges act as counterweights and the gate becomes a fence
once more.

Places of interest in the Neighbourhood
  2. The Riot Trial Salver (Bridgwater)
36. Site Of The Last Battle In England (Westonzoyland)

Food and Accommodation
Both available in Bridgwater

24 Where Criminals Sought Sanctuary

Position: The Priory Church of St Andrew, Stogursey
Ordnance Map: Weston-super-Mare & Bridgwater area; Sheet 182
1:50 000
Map Ref: ST 2045/4280

Note: Almost at floor level, in the church on the south arch, facing west, is a large ring. Known as a Sanctuary Ring, it dates back to the 13th century, to a time when criminals seeking to evade rough justice sought sanctuary within the church. Anyone violating sanctuary to capture a refugee was liable to severe punishment.

The right to sanctuary predates Christianity when the holiest sites in the pagan religion were deemed to impart holiness to their visitors. Roman law included Christian places of worship in AD 419, and sanctuary extended as far as 50 paces from the church door. Those accused of a felony could claim sanctuary for up to forty days, within which time the fugitive was required to choose between standing trial or making full confession of his offence, forfeiting his possessions and leaving the country until such time as the sovereign would allow him to return. In a few places fugitives could claim lifelong sanctuary, but by the time of the Reformation there was much abuse of the right and new laws reduced the protection afforded. In 1643 the custom was abolished in most places and, by the end of that century, sanctuary no longer was permitted.

The ring at St Andrew's Priory was installed after a murderer, one John de Rechich, was granted sanctuary and then absconded before his trial in 1243, leaving the priory liable for his fine. Subsequent fugitives were tethered to the ring until their cases had been heard or until they had confessed their crime to a coroner.

Places of interest in the Neighbourhood
   8. Site Of A Victorian Scandal (Four Forks)
  10. Where Somerset Was Going To Rival Texas (Kilve)
  30. The Port That Was (Lilstock)
  63. The Hunted Weathercock (Bicknoller)

Food and Accommodation
Food available in the vicinity; accommodation at Bridgwater

25 A Gift Of A Swedish MP

Position: Minehead
Ordnance Map: Minehead and Brendon Hills; Sheet 181 1:50 000
Map Ref: SS 9700/4640
Access: Make for St Andrew's Church, Wellington Square, in the centre
of Minehead (the town centre road off the A39 goes straight to the
square). The statue of Queen Anne stands in front of the church.

Note: Jacob Bancks, a Swede by birth, was a Royal Navy captain. Mary
Luttrell was widowed in 1690 by the death of her husband Col Francis
Luttrell. Capt Bancks rescued Mary from a disastrous fire at her London
home, and not long after they were married. In 1698 Jacob was elected
Member of Parliament for Minehead and served the borough until 1713;
he was knighted in 1699. Bancks was a great admirer of Queen Anne; he
saw her statue at the West Front of St Paul's Cathedral in London, and in
1719 commissioned the sculptor, Francis Bird, to make a similar one for
Minehead. The effigy was set up in St Michael's Church, but was
removed in 1880 when the church was restored. Plans fell through to
place Queen Anne in the new Town Hall and eventually, in 1893, the
townspeople subscribed to defray the cost of a canopy and the re-erection
of the statue at its present site.

Places of interest in the Neighbourhood
31. The Stone Beehive (Allerford)
42. The Houses Protected By A Curse (Minehead)
52. The Oldest Dovecote In England? (Blackford)

26 The 'Lady Shrine' That Is No Lady

Position: On West Bagborough Hill
Ordnance Map: Minehead and Brendon Hills; Sheet 181 1:50 000
Map Ref: ST 1790/3350
Access: From the A358 take the road to West Bagborough, continue through the village, passing Higher House on your right, and follow the road until you reach Tilbury Farm. The 'Lady Shrine' is inside a field on the right side of the road.

Note: Local legend has it that the statue standing facing across the hillside towards the site of Cothelstone House is a headless statue of Our Lady that at one time was a shrine. Seen from the road, the figure does indeed appear to be headless, but examination from the other side shows that the carving is that of a man, naked save for a cloak. At his feet is the crude representation of a dog. The statue, and the half-ruined red

sandstone summer house on a rise nearby (said by the legend to be a ruined chapel), are believed to have been placed in position by Thomas Slocombe, the owner of Tirhill House during the late 18th century. He followed the vogue of the time and included follies in the landscaping of his estate. The house was demolished by the Esdailes, who built Cothelstone House on the site; now that house too has gone, leaving only the follies in place.

Places of interest in the Neighbourhood
6. Is The Font Inverted? (Lydeard St Lawrence)
14. The Hill Surveyed By Schoolboys (Wills Neck)

Food and Accommodation
Plenty of both available in Taunton; in Bishops Lydeard, the Lethbridge Arms and the Bell Inn both have an excellent menu.

27 The Strange Building

Position: Doulting
Ordnance Map: Yeovil to Frome; Sheet 183 1:50 000
Map Ref: ST 6480/4315
Access: On the left side of the A361 from Shepton Mallet, not far from the village sign is a stile and just beyond that, tucked into a corner of a field, is the building.

Note: There's a wealth of written material on Doulting, its church and St Aldhelm's Well, but apart from an unspecified circle on a map, I could find no mention of the solidly built stone building that resembles nothing so much as a lock-up. That it was no lock-up seemed obvious – it is away from the centre of the village; hauling an inebriated troublemaker over the stile would have been most awkward. The fact that the opening to the building was on the other side of a garden wall also eliminated the possibility of it being a village overnight gaol, and the suggestion that it might cover a well was dismissed because it is on top of the hill. Several telephone calls, culminating in one to John Todd the owner of the Manor House (and of the little building), solved the mystery. It's a little folly or gazebo, but as it faces north northeast it's not the most salubrious of spots from which to admire the garden. Mr Todd believes it was built in the second half of the 19th century as a decorative means of filling in the top corner of the garden. Nowadays, and probably almost since it was built, the gazebo is used to store winter feed for the steers that graze the field; in January and February the animals come right up to the door to get their daily rations. Mr Todd installed the stile to help walkers, as there is a footpath that leads down the hill to a gate beside the bridlepath at the bottom.

Places of interest in the Neighbourhood
57. Fifteenth Century Market Stalls (Shepton Mallet)
61. The Stream That Powered Thirty Mills (Shepton Mallet and Doulting)
69. The Grave Shown On The Map (East Compton)

Food and Accommodation
Both available in Shepton Mallet; there is also an hotel at Doulting, but it may be advisable to book accommodation in advance

28 Nunney's Moving Cross

Position: Nunney
Ordnance Map: Yeovil to Frome; Sheet 183 1:50 000
Map Ref: ST 7375/4570
Access: The cross is on the castle side of the road, near a pond and opposite the parish church

Note: The stone cross was originally located in the churchyard, and at that time was not so elaborate in design. During the mid-19th century, the sound of children playing up and down the steps at the base so annoyed the rector that in 1869 he had the cross removed. Several years later the squire of nearby Whatley, J. H. Shore, recognised the stones in a local mason's yard and bought them for £2. He engaged an architect to restore the cross, and to add a Celtic head, then set it up in the grounds of his home. In 1959 after his death and the demolition by fire of his home, the people of Nunney raised sufficient money to buy back and re-erect the cross. Unfortunately, the site in the churchyard was by then occupied by a grave, so the cross was set up between church and castle.

Places of interest in the Neighbourhood
  9. The Horse In The Church (Mells)
 75. The Mini-Follies Of Frome
 77. The Church In The Farmyard (Hardington Bampfylde)

Food and Accommodation
Both available at Nunney, but if the hotel is fully booked, go to Frome.

29 Shades Of Industrial Somerset

Position: Brendon Hill
Ordnance Map: Minehead and Brendon Hills; Sheet 181 1:50 000
Map Ref: ST 0245/3445
Access: Drive along the road linking Raleigh's Cross with Wheddon
Cross and the remains of the Brendon Hill incline are on the north side,
about a quarter of a mile from the little chapel at the road fork.

Note: Industrial decline is not a new phenomenon of this century; more
than 100 years ago, the countryside around Brendon Hill was dotted
with mines and a railway kept several locomotives working carrying iron
ore to the busy little port of Watchet. The village of Brendon Hill
contained 60 cottages, housing a population of about 250. Two
establishments sold coal and building materials to the community, a
general store offered dry goods and tradesmen visited the village
regularly. There was no public house in the village, Raleigh's Cross Inn
was near enough to satisfy the needs of those who wanted strong drink,
but a Mr Brown set up a Temperance House (which later became a
general shop known as Davis's Stores). The Beulah Chapel at the road
fork was opened by the Bible Christians in 1861, the Wesleyans
worshipped in a chapel over the stable at the mine manager's house, and
the Anglicans had their Iron Church that served also as the village school
from 1861. The railway flourished, carrying not only the ore trains but
also some 19,000 passengers from Comberow to Watchet and back in
1872.

The village came about after the Enclosures Acts had enabled wealthy
men to fence off vast tracts of land and begin digging to see what lay
beneath the surface. There were a number of independent mines on the
Brendons and as the pace of industry quickened so did interest deepen in
exploiting the mineral wealth to feed it. In 1853, Thomas Brown of the
Ebbw Vale ironworks formed the Brendon Hills Iron Ore Co. after
gaining control of several small mines. The ore was carried by horse and
cart to Watchet and shipped across to Wales. Permission was granted in
1855 to construct the West Somerset Mineral Railway from Watchet
harbour via Roadwater to Brendon Hill; eventually it was extended to
Gupworthy. The first sod was turned in May 1856 and in April 1857 the
first ore was shipped by rail from Roadwater to Watchet. The line
reached Comberow in December 1857, but as the railway had to
negotiate an incline of 1 in 4 between Comberow and Brendon Hill,

work on that section was not finished until 1861. Output rose steadily, reaching 40,000 tons annually during the 1874-78 period. Then Spanish ore dropped dramatically in price, forcing closure of the more costly British mines. Trade revived, but by 1883 all production had ceased. There was another short revival from 1907 to 1910 with limited production of 2,550 tons in 1908.

Now, only the manager's house, Sea View, remains intact along with the one-time shop. You can visit the remains of the winding house that once contained machinery to haul the train up the steep incline, but take care – it is not a place for the very young or the disabled to scramble about.

Places of interest in the Neighbourhood
53. The Inn That Was Also A Tollhouse (Hungerford)
59. The Dovecote With A Revolving Ladder (Dunster)

Food and Accommodation
Food available at Raleigh's Cross Inn and at Wheddon Cross; accommodation at Dunster.

30 The Port That Was

Position: Lilstock
Ordnance Map: Minehead and Brendon Hills; Sheet 181 1:50 000
Map Ref: ST 1715/4535
Access: Take the Kilton road north off the A39 where the road makes a right-hand bend between Holford and Kilve; bear left at Kilton church and follow the road past another church, bearing right until you see the sign to the left pointing to the parking lot.

Note: Anyone interested in industrial archaeology will find this place very exciting (see also 29 and 70). Lilstock was developed as a port in the 19th century. About 1820, Sir John Acland, a local landowner, built a boathouse on the beach near the stream and from this developed a cross-channel trade. Coal was imported from Wales for the Aclands' domestic use at Fairfield and to fire a limekiln on the cliff, and pit props were exported. By 1848 the port had grown sufficiently to have resident coastguards and by 1855 a customs officer had joined the community. A stone pier was added about 1860 and by 1886 there were warehouses under the cliff beside the southern harbour wall. The Board of Admiralty two years later considered a plan for a canal terminal at Lilstock with Seaton at the other end but nothing came of the idea. During the 1860s and 1870s pleasure steamers included Lilstock among their ports of call. Soon after the end of the 1914-18 War the pier was destroyed because the harbour had been abandoned. Today, the entrance to the harbour is blocked by tons and tons of pebbles; vegetation covers the massive stone blocks that formed the harbour wall and you have to push through bushes and nettles to see the chambers that formed part of the warehouses (they were so sturdily built that several still have roofs). Traces can be found of steps that led down from the quay and rusting metal shows where once lockgates prevented docked vessels capsizing with the falling tide.

Places of interest in the Neighbourhood
10. Where Somerset Was Going To Rival Texas (Kilve)
18. The Village Where Time Seems To Stand Still (East Quantoxhead)

Food and Accommodation
Food available along the A39; accommodation available at Minehead

31 The Stone Beehive

Position: Allerford
Ordnance Map: Minehead and Brendon Hills; Sheet 181 1:50 000
Map Ref: ST 9050/4675
Access: Park beside the north side of the A39 opposite Piles Mill; then walk the few yards to where the A39 crosses a stream – the 'beehive' is near the east bank.

Note: The beehive-shaped stone structure, now much overgrown with vegetation, is believed to be medieval and at one time was reputed to be an ash house in which potash from the bake ovens was stored for use on kitchen gardens in springtime. Tourists enquiring as to its origin were told it was a pixy house; some folk speculated that it had been intended as a pig-stye, because there were similarly shaped, but larger, structures for pigs at Berrow. Recently it has been discovered that the 'beehive' was a dipping well. Water from the stream was purified as it percolated through the gravel floor and, in the days before the parish pump was installed, village housewives could bring their buckets and dip out the day's water supply from the well.

Places of interest in the Neighbourhood
25. The Gift Of A Swedish MP (Minehead)
42. The Houses Protected By A Curse (Minehead)
52. The Oldest Dovecote In England? (Blackford)
80. The Steepest Motorable Hill in England (Porlock)

Food and Accommodation
Good choice of both available at Minehead

32 Printed In Germany

Position: Chard Museum
Ordnance Map: Taunton and Lyme Regis; Sheet 193 1:50 000
Map Ref: ST 3190/0870
Access: The museum is located beside the A30 at the Honiton end of the town

Note: There is no indication of the purpose for which it was intended, but an Ordnance Survey 1 inch to the mile map of the Chard and Axminster district, printed with English place names and measurements, but otherwise in German, was handed in at the door of Chard Museum one day. It is dated 1941, hence is too late for the planned invasion of England; it would seen to be insufficiently detailed to be of much use in targeting industries for bombing and is also unsuited to folding small for concealment from guards in the event of the carrier being captured and sent to this particular area of England. So unless someone who was involved with the printing and knows the reasons for it steps forward, it is likely to remain one of those unsolved mysteries belonging to the war years.

Places of interest in the Neighbourhood
16. The Brass That Became A Soap Advert (Crewkerne)

Food and Accommodation
Both available at Chard

33 The Littlest Sunday School

Position: Frome
Ordnance Map: Yeovil to Frome; Sheet 183 1:50 000
Map Ref: ST 7775/4840
Access: Park in the centre of Frome in the car-park near the information centre. Walk out of the car-park and turn right as though to go up the hill. A footpath is signposted to the left (up a steep hill). Follow that and on your left you will see the Zion United Reformed Church. Go round the outside of the building (in Whittox Lane) and in through the gates and the littlest Sunday School is in the grounds to the right.

Note: This little octagonal building dates from 1875. Its purpose was forgotten for quite a while after it ceased to be used, but when it was opened recently it was found to be a Sunday School, complete with benches, for the pupils of the old Zion Church. As it would not have accommodated many children, and as there were several rooms within the main church building that would have been suitable for Sunday School use, it has been suggested that the littlest Sunday School was an early kindergarten or creche, built to cut down on disturbance to the adults worshipping in the church.

Zion Church was built in 1810. It was an offshoot of the Rook Lane Chapel (built in 1707 and considered by many to be the finest surviving non-conformist chapel in England), which itself was founded when those who could not accept the 1662 Prayer Book and the Act of Uniformity broke away from the Established Church to form a Congregational church. Now things have gone full circle; the Rook Lane community has joined the Zion group and the Old Rook Lane Chapel is to be used for secular purposes.

Places of interest in the Neighbourhood
  9. The Horse In The Church (Mells)
75. The Mini-Follies Of Frome
77. The Church In The Farmyard (Hardington Bampfylde)

Food and Accommodation
Both available in Frome

34 The Dog Pound (And Why It Was Built)

Position: Holford
Ordnance Map: Minehead and Brendon Hills; Sheet 181 1:50 000
Map Ref: ST 1545/4110
Access: In Holford take the road west off the A39 at the Plough Inn, and follow the road, keeping right at the fork, toward Alfoxton Park Hotel. The pound stands beside the road in a wooded area at the next junction.

Note: Dorothy and William Wordsworth rented Alfoxton House for one year, from July 1797 until June 1798, by arrangement with the agent in the absence of the owners (who were most annoyed when they heard – the Wordsworths were definitely not of the right social class for Alfoxton!) The Wordsworths would have seen the local foxhounds being exercised daily by the huntsman, but whether the Dog Pound was in existence then is uncertain.

It was customary, in the days before refrigeration, to store meat for the foxhounds by hanging it in the branches of trees near to the kennels. Stray dogs were attracted to the larder and would congregate at night in an attempt to reach the meat. The hounds, of course, would set up a commotion at the presence of these strangers. One night, the racket became so intense that the kennelman of the time got out of bed and threw on a few clothes so that he might go and silence the howling. He

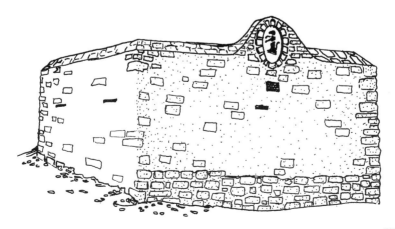

took his whip to the kennels, but neglected to put on his everyday coat. No one knew exactly what happened, but it is assumed that when he reached his hounds they failed to recognise him without the smell of the old familiar jacket and so they tore him apart. The Dog Pound is said to have been built so that stray animals could be rounded up and kept there until claimed by their owners. There is a local tradition that the ghost of the kennelman, torn and bloodied, can be seen walking the hills at night.

The enclosure is large enough to allow for cows and sheep also to be impounded. The slits that are on two sides of the enclosure are of a height that would allow a man seated on a horse to look in and identify his animal.

The pound was given to the village of Holford in 1982 by the family of the late John Lancelot Brereton, descendants of the St Albyns, owners of Alfoxton since the 15th century. The crest of the family appears on the front of the pound.

Places of interest in the Neighbourhood
10. Where Somerset Was Going To Rival Texas (Kilve)
18. The Village Where Time Seems To Stand Still (East Quantoxhead)
24. Where Criminals Sought Sanctuary (Stogursey)

Food and Accommodation
Food available locally; accommodation at Minehead or Bridgwater

35 Rival Towers

Position: Ammerdown House
Ordnance Map: Yeovil to Frome; Sheet 183 1:50 000
Map Ref: ST 7190/5215
Access: A footpath leads to The Column from Buckland Down, but the
Faulkland Tower and its cottages were demolished in 1969.

Note: Thomas Samuel Jolliffe was a wealthy landowner and an MP;
when he died aged 78 in 1824, his bachelor son, a lieutenant colonel in
the Somerset Militia, inherited the estate. In 1853, moved perhaps by a
long-dormant wish to commemorate his father's memory, John Jolliffe
commissioned Joseph Jopling, a civil engineer and architect to begin
work on The Column, a tower built on a hill so that its glass-domed top
would be 700ft above sea level (the tower is about 110ft high). A year
later the colonel died and his younger brother, the 73-year old Rev
Thomas Robert Jolliffe, finished building The Column.

Thomas Robert died without issue and the estate passed to the Hyltons
who were direct descendants of Thomas Samuel's sister. Lord Hylton
was a very shy man. A local quarry owner, one John Turner, failed in a
lawsuit against Lord Hylton and, knowing of his shyness, determined to
do such damage as he could in another direction. Accordingly he built a
tower on his own land in the village of Faulkland; to help make it pay, at
the base he placed a dance hall and tea garden, counting no doubt on the
custom of local miners and their families. Reports as to the date vary
(1885, 1891) as do reports of the height of the structure (150ft up to
180ft); it is known that the top 30ft of the tower was of wood, and that
Mr Turner would mount to the top to look over into his enemy's parkland
and watch the comings and goings at the house. The tea gardens and
dance hall were unsuccessful. Turner died in 1894 aged 75; Lord Hylton
bought the tower and dance hall, but before he could begin to demolish
the tower, the wooden section was destroyed by lightning. Most of the
tower was taken down, and the stump and dance hall were turned into
cottages for estate workers. Photos from 1955 show the strange-looking
group to have been somewhat unattractive, and its demolition in 1969
was no loss to the appearance of the community.

Places of interest in the Neighbourhood
  9. The Horse In The Church (Mells)
 77. The Church In The Farmyard (Hardington Bampfylde)

Food and Accommodation
Food available in Tucker's Grave Inn at Faulkland, and accommodation
can be found in Frome

36 Site Of The Last Battle In England

Position: Westonzoyland
Ordnance Map: Weston-super-Mare & Bridgwater area; Sheet 182
1:50 000
Map Ref: ST 3505/3575
Access: The site of the battlefield is signposted within the town

Note: In the early hours of July 6 1685, across a swampy section of
King's Sedgemoor on the Somerset Levels, the government forces of the
Catholic James II fought the Protestant rebel force led by James, Duke of
Monmouth, illegitimate son of Charles II. The government forces,
better led, better trained and better equipped, won the day at the Battle of
Sedgemoor – the men of the West Country gave James's men a tough
time but it was all over by 8 am. Afterwards, James took his revenge on
the survivors of the battle; many were hanged as a result of the infamous
Bloody Assizes, conducted in various towns by Judge Jeffreys; others
were transported for life, torn from their families and friends for fighting
for a cause they believed in. Monmouth was executed on Tower Hill, but
Jeffreys himself also died in the Tower (in 1689) – where he had been
imprisoned following the overthrow in 1688 of James by William of
Orange. Today that section of Sedgemoor probably looks much as it did
in the 17th century – deserted and somewhat eerie – the fight to keep the
Protestant faith for England is commemorated by a stone bearing the
following inscription:

In memory of all those who
Doing the right as they gave it
Fell in the Battle of Sedgemoor
6th July 1685
And lie buried in this field
Or, who for their share in this fight
Suffered death
Punishment or transportation
PRO PATRIA

The stone is surrounded by four staddlestones; each bears a different date: 1600, Sedgemoor 1685; 1700, Plassey 1757 Quebec 1759; 1800, Trafalgar 1805 Waterloo 1815; 1900, Great War 1914-18 2nd World War 1939-45. Somerset men have never been slow to come forward to 'do the right as they gave it.'

Places of interest in the Neighbourhood
2. The Riot Trial Salver (Bridgwater)
23. The Never Open Gate (Chedzoy)
38. The Cast-Iron Milepost (Greinton)
40. Monument To An Admiral (Butleigh)

Food and Accommodation
Food available at Westonzoyland; accommodation at Bridgwater

37 The Case Of The Missing Body

Position: Wheal Eliza Mine, near Simonsbath
Ordnance Map: Barnstaple and Ilfracombe; Sheet 180 1:50 000
Map Ref: SS 7855/3810
Access: A footpath south off the B3223 at Simonsbath follows the River Barle and leads past Winstitchen Farm to Wheal Eliza Cottage and the disused mine in about one mile.

Note: The story of William Burgess begins with the meeting in 1846 of five men, John Knight, landowner, and four others, all hopeful of making money. John Knight owned vast tracts of land on Exmoor that he was seeking to develop; the other four agreed to employ at least six miners at a site known to hold a large deposit of copper, and to pay John Knight 15% of the value of the ore removed, minus the cost of transportation. Once 200 tons of ore had been removed, the four agreed to build housing for the miners. Thus was founded the Wheal Eliza Mine at Cow Castle. Ore was removed for only a short while before the mine became uneconomic and was allowed to flood.

William Burgess lived with his family at Whitewater. In 1857 his wife died, leaving him with three children. Tom and Emma were no problem – he put them out to service at a North Molton farm – but Anna was too young to work. Burgess took her with him when he went into lodgings with a Mrs Marley at Gallon House Cot near Simonsbath. Burgess was a heavy drinker and was soon short of money. He persuaded the local parson, a man named Thornton, to help him make good the loss of a pony and a pig by writing a brief for him. Briefs were a common means by which poor folk approached those better off for financial assistance. Burgess soon drank away the money raised, and by doing so he incurred the wrath of Parson Thornton. It wasn't long before Burgess found that the half crown he was paying each week for Anna's keep might be put to better use. One Sunday in June 1858, he told his landlady that he was taking the child to live with her grandmother and set off, carrying with him Anna's spare clothing. That evening he returned without the child. The following Thursday he too left.

Not long after, someone noticed a pile of burnt clothing behind Gallon House Inn and Mrs Marley identified an unburnt scrap of calico as belonging to Anna's spare frock. Parson Thornton heard of it and he sent to discover whether Anna was with her grandmother – she was not – whereupon he organised a search of the moors and himself rode to Curry

Rivel to fetch the chief of police. When the two men returned, the searchers reported that they had found a recently dug shallow grave but no body. Sheep stealers enter the story here. At that time, after stealing and killing a sheep, it was usual to bury the animal until a market had been found for the meat and then to return and disinter the evidence. Sheep stealers had noticed the grave on the Tuesday after Anna's 'departure' and by some quirk of fate had mentioned it (thinking another sheep thief had been at work in 'their' patch) to Burgess. Realising he had no time to lose, Burgess removed Anna's body from the grave and had then thrown her into the shaft of the flooded mine. Two days later he took ship across the Bristol Channel and vanished into the streets of Swansea. Parson Thornton guessed where he had gone and not long after the grave was found, Burgess was arrested and taken to prison in Dulverton. In his pockets were found Anna's boots, but not a word would he say as to her whereabouts. The search went on through July and August and the magistrates were about to release the father for lack of the body when a man came forward with the evidence that hanged Burgess. He had been on the moors on nefarious business on the Tuesday and although he had seen nothing, had heard someone going towards the Wheal Eliza Mine. The Dulverton magistrates immediately ordered the mine to be drained, no small task seeing that the shaft went 360ft into the earth, and they guaranteed the cost of pumping should no body be found. It took until November and cost £350 to drain the mine and a young man then volunteered to go down and see what he could find. He returned bearing a tarpaulin bag inside which were Anna's remains. Burgess was hanged on January 4 1859 at Taunton Gaol.

Places of interest in the Neighbourhood
15. The Village Where Eight Bridges Aren't Enough (Winsford)
25. A Gift Of A Swedish MP (Minehead)
42. The Houses Protected By A Curse (Minehead)

Food and Accommodation
During the tourist season, finding good food is no problem. There are hotels at Simonsbath and Exford, and several farms in the area offer bed and breakfast, but without advance booking, you will probably be better advised to make for a larger centre such as Minehead for accommodation.

38 The Cast-Iron Milepost

Position: Greinton
Ordnance Map: Weston-super-Mare & Bridgwater area; Sheet 182
1:50 000
Map Ref: ST 4077/3617
Access: Look for the post on the northwest side of the A361 near the
western outskirts of Greinton

Note: This is the only known highway milepost in Somerset to have been
cast in iron. It is post-turnpike in date – that is, after 1862 – and was
made at the Bridgwater foundry of Messrs J. Culverwell & Co. It would
seem from the measurements, that the surveyor of that time was most
anxious to be as precise as possible.

Places of interest in the Neighbourhood
47. Gracie Fields' First Clogs (Street)
55. The Church That Became A War Memorial (Burrow Mump)
68. Was This Where Alfred Burnt Those Cakes? (Athelney)

Food and Accommodation
Both available at Street and at Bridgwater

39 A Painted Chimneypiece

Position: Barrington Court
Ordnance Map: Taunton and Lyme Regis; Sheet 193 1:50 000
Map Ref: ST 4000/1820
Access: At Barrington, off the B3168, follow the National Trust signs
for Barrington Court.

Note: Although Barrington Court is owned by The National Trust, it is
leased to Andrew Lyle, who in turn has leased part of it to Stuart Interiors
as a showroom for the company's period and reproduction furniture, all
of which is for sale. On the first floor is a room, presumed to have been
the best parlour during the early 17th century, that contains a rare
example of a painted stone chimneypiece. It dates from about 1625
when the house was owned by a Spanish merchant of Shepton Mallet,
one William Strode (not the William Strode who was indicted for high
treason in 1642). His wife was Joan Barnard, heiress to Downside, and
the centre panel of the painting contains the coats of arms of both the
Strode and Barnard families. The outside panels have been described as
showing Byzantine 6th and 7th century influence, but nothing is known
of the artist.

Places of interest in the Neighbourhood
17. The Tower Built By A Prime Minister (Curry Rivel)
22. This Clock Has Ten Faces – And Still Is Inaccurate (Barrington
     Court)

Food and Accommodation
Food available in Barrington; food and accommodation can be found in
Taunton, nine miles away

40 Monument To An Admiral

Position: Hood Monument (Windmill Hill) Great Breach Wood
Ordnance Map: Weston-super-Mare & Bridgwater area; Sheet 182
1:50 000
Map Ref: ST 5025/3165
Access: Take the B3153, Somerton/Keinton Mandeville road to
Christian's Cross (2 miles northeast of Somerton), take the northwest
turning to Wickham's Cross and on the left side, about half a mile past
the turning to Butleigh is a track leading into woods; follow that and you
will reach the obelisk.

Note: The Hoods originated at Mosterton in Dorset (where their family
home is now the Admiral Hood pub), but John Hood migrated to
Butleigh in the 17th century and founded a dynasty that produced several
famous naval men about the same time. Vice Admiral Sir Samuel Hood,
Bt (1762-1814), son of Samuel Hood, was the most famous, but father
Samuel's uncle (another Samuel), vicar of Butleigh from 1723 to 1761,
had three sons, two of whom also became admirals (Samuel, Admiral
Lord Hood 1724-1816 and Alexander, Admiral Lord Bridport 1724-
1814) – the third son took Holy Orders and became vicar of Butleigh
when his father died. The Hood monument commemorates the Vice
Admiral and is described as a 'Tuscan column with a drum with heavily
framed circular openings, topped by a glass dome and big stone shields'
– but it is more likely that the 'shields' are supposed to represent sails.
The column dominates the countryside, despite the many mature trees
that now surround it.

Places of interest in the Neighbourhood
47. Gracie Fields' First Clogs (Street)

Food and Accommodation
Both available in Street and Somerton

41 The Chapel Above The Road

Position: Langport
Ordnance Map: Taunton and Lyme Regis; Sheet 193 1:50 000
Map Ref: ST 4260/2655
Access: The Hanging Chapel is located at the Huish Episcopi side of the
town; although it is kept locked, it is possible to view the chapel by
applying either to Mr Richard J. Stranger (Tel: Langport 251610), or to
Mr W. J. Dagworthy (Tel: Langport 250702).

Note: The Hanging Chapel originated in the 13th century but is mainly
of 15th century work; it was restored in the 19th century. The first
written record that survives dates from 1344 when the building was a

chantry chapel dedicated to the Blessed Virgin Mary. From 1596 to 1600 it served as Langport's Town Hall. Langport Grammar School was housed there from 1706 until about 1790. After such auspicious uses, the place was leased to private individuals. It became an arms store for the local militia from 1809 to 1816, a Sunday school from 1818 to 1827 then it returned to private leasing. From 1834 until 1875 the Chapel housed stuffed birds collected by Edward Quekett, a microscopist and one of three Langport brothers, sons of William Quekett who was a clergyman, author and one-time headmaster of the Grammar School. Edward Quekett's collection contained rare moorland birds and a number of species that are now extinct. With the closure of the museum, the Chapel again was leased privately for a while. Since 1891 it has been leased to a masonic order for use as a lodge and has added protection in that it is now classed as an Ancient Monument.

Places of interest in the Neighbourhood
17. The Tower Built By A Prime Minister (Burton Pynsent)
45. The Barrel Organ And The Buxom Angels (Muchelney)
65. When Langport Had Trains (And Floods)

Food and Accommodation
Both available in Langport; if accommodation is fully booked, Bridgwater is about ten miles away

42 The Houses Protected By A Curse

Position: Minehead
Ordnance Map: Minehead and Brendon Hills; Sheet 181 1:50 000
Map Ref: SS 9680/4640
Access: The Quirke Almshouses are in Market House Lane round the
corner from The Information Centre on The Parade.

Note: The almshouses have recently been restored and modernised –
possibly because of a curse. In the 17th century, Robert Quirke, a master
mariner, was caught in a severe storm at sea while returning from an
outward journey to deliver a cargo of herrings. His ship was carrying a
mixed cargo for the homeward trip and so severe was the storm that he
and his crew vowed that, if they survived, they would sell the ship and
her cargo for the benefit of the poor. As a result, eleven almshouses were
built on the site of an old market place (the stump of the market cross is
still there); some of the ship's timbers were incorporated into the
buildings and the ship's bell was mounted above the end house. Over the
years, despite altering the houses first to make eight dwellings and later
to six, the endowment ran out. Thomas Ponsford, chairman of the Urban
District Council at the end of the 19th century, gave £3,000 towards the
upkeep and maintenance of the inmates but eventually that proved
insufficient and by 1983 the cottages were deemed unfit for further
habitation.

However, a plaque on the wall in the centre of the row reads:

> Robert Qvrke, sonne of Jame Qvrke
> Built this house ano: 1630: and
> Doth give it to vse of the poore
> Of this parish for ever and for better
> Maintenance doe give my two inner
> Sellers at the inner end of the key
> And cvrssed bee that man that shall
> Convert it to any other vse that to
> The vse of the poore: 1630
> God's Providence
> Is my Inheritance
> R.Q.
> E

It seems that none of the district councillors at Minehead was prepared, even in the 20th century, to risk bringing that curse on his (or her) head. Fortunately, an anonymous donor came forward and offered £120,000 towards renovation of the cottages, and the remaining £30,000 was forthcoming from the council. All the best of the original structure has been preserved, and to it has been added the amenities of modern living, including individual alarm systems for each cottage.

Places of interest in the Neighbourhood
25. The Gift Of A Swedish MP (Minehead)
80. The Steepest Motorable Hill In England (Porlock)

Food and Accommodation
Good choice of both available in Minehead

43 The Panel That Toppled A Religious Order

Position: In Templecombe Parish Church
Ordnance Map: Yeovil to Frome; Sheet 183 1:50 000
Map Ref: ST 7090/2175
Access: The key to the church is kept at the Rectory; a map in the porch shows how to get there

Note: During the 1939-45 War, a cottage in West Court, just off the High Street in Templecombe, was rented to a Mrs M. Drew. She was in the outhouse collecting wood one day when she happened to glance up and caught sight of a painted face looking down at her through the broken plaster of the ceiling. Investigation showed that the painting was on a wooden panel that had been tied into the roof with wire and then had been hidden by plaster. The face is that of a bearded man with rather full cheeks and a slightly open mouth. The painting is thought to date from the beginning of the 13th century and to have been connected with the Knights Templar, a religious order that acquired the manor in 1185 (hence the name Templecombe) to establish a preceptory. Remains of old Templar buildings can be seen at the Manor House. The order was suppressed in 1312 because members were accused, among other things, of idolatory – of worshipping a strange image. Almost every portrayal of Christ at that time showed Him with a halo; the Templars worshipped Him without a halo, and it has been suggested that the Knights brought the Holy Shroud to Europe during the time of the crusades and that they copied their painting from it. After the suppression, someone obviously hid the painting; at some time it may have been used as a door – a keyhole and hingemarks indicate such use.

In 1956, the owner of the cottage, Mrs A. Topp, presented the panel to the church. The painting was cleaned and restored and, more recently, placed in a case covered with shatter-proof glass.

Places of interest in the Neighbourhood
  3. The Man Who Built His Own Monument (Wincanton)
  5. The Gaol Built With Funds Filched From The Poor (Castle Cary)
56. Road Taxes Of The Past (South Cheriton)

Food and Accommodation
Both available at Wincanton

44 Where A Saxon George Fights His Dragon

Position: Stoke-sub-Hamdon
Ordnance Map: Taunton and Lyme Regis; Sheet 193 1:50 000
Map Ref: ST 4705/1595
Access: The Church of St Mary can be easily seen from the A303 or the A3088 and it is located on a small road that links the two highways

Note: On the north side of the exterior of the church, close to the west end of the building is an arch carved into one block of stone. The block is decorated with a man and a dragon that Pevsner describes as looking 'more Saxon than Norman' – certainly it is unlike any of the conventional carvings of this country's patron saint.

Places of interest in the Neighbourhood
  7. Tom Coryate's Much Travelled Shoes (Odcombe)
53. The Head Under The Seat (And The Dial Over The Porch) (Middle Chinnock)

Food and Accommodation
Food obtainable at the Muddled Man, West Chinnock and the Cat Head, Chiselborough. Accommodation available in Yeovil and Crewkerne.

45 The Barrel Organ And The Buxom Angels

Position: Church of St Peter and St Paul, Muchelney
Ordnance Map: Taunton and Lyme Regis; Sheet 193 1:50 000
Map Ref: ST 4290/2495
Access: At the crossroads in Muchelney; parking on the village green

Note: Muchelney is most famed for its ancient abbey ruins and for the
few ecclesiastical buildings that remained after the abbey closed in 1538
– it was not dissolved by Henry VIII, the monks departed of their own
free will. The parish church is worth visiting because not only does it
contain a church barrel organ (the last one known to be in the church
where it was installed when new – and that is still in working order), but
it also has a splendidly buxom set of angels painted on its wooden
ceiling. The angels date from the early 17th century. Originally there
were twelve large and twelve smaller panels to the ceiling, but in the
mid-19th century two sets of panels were damaged by time and damp
and fell out and the replacements are somewhat out of keeping. The
angels are not attired in the orthodox flowing white robes of such beings,
but wear costumes of the late 16th, early 17th centuries; the dresses of
four in particular are very *décolleté*, and several look quite surprised to
find themselves in such august surroundings. The barrel organ represents
a 19th century attempt to bring music into a church that had no competent
musicians (or maybe insufficient instruments) to lead the singing. Built
by Messrs Gray & Davison about 1835-40, it was used regularly until
1870, with a choice of 25 hymn tunes and three double chants, and in its
time the organ was probably considered a very elegant little instrument
with its oak casing and gilt pipe front.

Places of interest in the Neighbourhood
22. This Clock Has Ten Faces – And Still Is Inaccurate (Barrington)
39. A Painted Chimneypiece (Barrington)
41. The Chapel Above The Road (Langport)
65. When Langport Had Trains (And Floods)

Food and Accommodation
Food available at Muchelney; accommodation at South Petherton

46 Three Manors For Three Daughters

Position: Preston Plucknett and Brympton D'Evercy
Ordnance Map: Yeovil to Frome; Sheet 183 1:50 000
Map Ref: ST 5350/1640
Access: Take the Taunton/Montacute road out of Yeovil and you will
soon come to Preston Plucknett; look for the Bartlett Construction
Company headquarters, which is housed in the Abbey Farm, on the
north side of the road.

Note: Preston Plucknett is named after Alan de Plugenet who was
granted the estate by Henry III in 1272. By 1300 the land had been sold
to John de Stourton who passed it to his son John (Jenkyn). This John
built the house that now stands on the site; he was Somerset's MP
between 1420 and 1435. He had no sons, but he did have three
daughters, and he also owned two other manors in the area, Brympton
D'Evercy and Pendomer. Daughter Joan received Brympton D'Evercy
on her marriage to John Sydenham, Alice had Pendomer when she
married William Daubeney and in 1436, on the death of her father,
Cecily inherited Preston Plucknett. Her son, John Hill, became the
owner following Cecily's death in 1472.

Through the ages, the manor changed hands several times and was leased to a number of tenants as a farm. In 1841, Lady Georgiana Fane (there are Ponsonby-Fanes at Brympton D'Evercy today) inherited the estate. She was a somewhat forceful, strongly opinionated lady, and she became convinced that the land had once belonged to a religious house and therefore was not subject to tithe payments. She changed the name to Abbey Farm and began proceedings against the Tithe Commissioners, but after spending five years and a fortune in litigation, she lost her case. The name has remained, however.

In 1969, the Bartlett Construction Company bought the property. The house and Tithe Barn are listed as Grade I protected buildings. The new owners have restored the fabric and have adapted the interior within the constraints of the Environment Department's guidelines to give the house and barn a new lease of useful life. The barn is used as a showroom for home improvement materials, so that it is possible to go inside; the manor houses the offices of the company. Brympton D'Evercy is open to the public and the tourist information offices in various part of Somerset have the relevant information.

Places of interest in the Neighbourhood
7. Tom Coryate's Much Travelled Shoes (Odcombe)
44. Where A Saxon George Fights His Dragon (Stoke-sub-Hamdon)
50. The Painted Doors Of St Mary's Church (Norton-sub-Hamdon)

Food and Accommodation
Both available in Yeovil

47 Gracie Fields' First Clogs

Position: Shoe Museum, Street
Ordnance Map: Weston-super-Mare & Bridgwater area; Sheet 182
1:50 000
Map Ref: ST 4840/3685
Access: Go into Street from the A39 and the museum is on the north side
of the High Street at the Glastonbury end of the town

Note: Gracie Fields was a well known entertainer whose career spanned
some fifty years. Her remarkable singing voice might have earned her an
operatic career, but she preferred to perform in the variety theatre. Born
in Rochdale in January 1898, she began appearing in local concerts in
1905 and by the time she was 17 she had left her job in the cotton mill to
join a touring company. Her first film, 'Sally in Our Alley', was made in

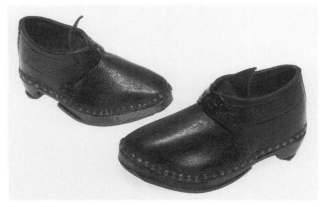

Gracie Fields' first clogs.

1931 and was a great success. By the mid-1930s Gracie Fields for a
while was the world's highest paid movie star. She left England in 1940
because her second husband, Monty Banks, was of Italian descent and
as such was considered an undesirable alien. They lived in the United
States and after the war returned to Europe to settle on the Isle of Capri.
In 1939 'Our Gracie' received the CBE and in 1979, shortly before her
death, she was made DBE. Her first clogs, made by Bob Brierley, a
Rochdale clogger, were presented to the Shoe Museum by Miss Fields'

Lady Diana Spencer's wedding shoes.

former companion.

Also in the museum are the shoes worn by Lady Diana Spencer on the day she married The Prince of Wales.

Places of interest in the Neighbourhood
38. The Cast-Iron Milepost (Greinton)
40. Monument To An Admiral (Butleigh)
55. The Church That Became A War Memorial (Burrow Mump)

Food and Accommodation
Both available at Street; also at Glastonbury

48 The Tower That's Made of Leather

Position: In Somerset County Museum, Taunton Castle
Ordnance Map: Taunton and Lyme Regis; Sheet 193 1:50 000
Map Ref: ST 2230/2455
Access: Taunton Castle is in the centre of the town and can be reached on foot from North Street through a gateway beside the SWEB showrooms, or from Corporation Street. There is a car park within the castle grounds for museum visitors.

Note: In 1858 rebuilding began of the tower of the Church of St Mary Magdalene in Taunton. A faithful copy in leather was made of the tower built during the years 1488 to 1514, and this copy was carried in the procession on August 3 1858 that heralded the laying of the foundation stone for the rebuilding. Newspaper reports of the day indicate that the inauguration of the new tower on September 8 1862 was a gala occasion celebrated by all the townspeople. There is mention of 'The Model of St Mary's Tower belonging to Mr Brannan' being borne by men in the procession on that occasion, but whether it was the leather model now displayed in the museum is impossible to discover.

Places of interest in the Neighbourhood
  1. One Of The Gems Of The Great Exhibition (Taunton)
72. Where Lepers Once Were Tended (Taunton)
78. The Toads That Children Love (Taunton)

Food and Accommodation
Both available in Taunton

49 The Strange Inscription

Position: Stawley
Ordnance Map: Minehead and Brendon Hills; Sheet 181 1:50 000
Map Ref: ST 0605/2265
Access: Go to St Michael's Church, which is at the end of a no-through road off the secondary road that connects the A38 near the Beam Bridge Inn with the A361 at Waterrow.

Note: The inscription is on the outside wall of the church under the West Window. It is very difficult to decipher, which is probably why each of the four authorities I consulted had a different version. All agree that the first three words are reversed, as though being read from the other side of a scroll, and after that it probably reads: Pray for the soules of Henry Howe and Agnes His Wyffe AD 1522 (1523).

While you are there, go inside the church through what must be one of the narrowest of church porches (who comes out first, the bride or the groom?) and see what a church that escaped the Victorian Gothic Revival looks like. The East Window is a rarity for its rectangular shape, there's a fine Georgian canopy over the pulpit and the North Window is a curiosity in itself as it is of a type brought over from Holland at the time of William and Mary. The failure of the church to be 'made over' by the Gothic Revivalists may be due to the Hayne family, father and two sons, who in turn were the rectors of Stawley from the 1840s to the end of the century. All were eccentrics and were reputed to go hunting wearing cassocks and brandishing umbrellas.

Places of interest in the Neighbourhood
21. At The Sign Of The Footless Bird (Langford Budville)
70. The Grand Canal That Wasn't So Grand (Nynehead)

Food and Accommodation
Both available at Wellington and at Taunton

50 The Painted Doors Of St Mary's Church

Position: Norton-sub-Hamdon
Ordnance Map: Taunton and Lyme Regis; Sheet 193 1:50 000
Map Ref: ST 4700/1600
Access: From the A303 take the B3165 and turn east into Norton-sub-Hamdon; the church is at the end of a cul-de-sac, but it is signposted.

Note: On July 29, 1894, the tower at the west end of the Church of the Blessed Virgin Mary at Norton-sub-Hamdon was struck by lightning, and despite the efforts of the parishioners to extinguish the blaze was devastated by fire. Plans for restoration were made immediately, and a year later to the day, a service was held to mark the completion of the work – a service that has been held annually on July 29 ever since. The tower was complete, but the West doors were temporary – a local resident had offered to bear the cost, but as the money had not been forthcoming, the salvaged timber intended for the doors still lay in a

nearby workshop. Eventually other funds were found and Arthur Parkin, a local craftsman, made the doors and decorated them with some delightful carvings of small animals as well as coats-of-arms of people associated in some way with the church. From left to right these are: Cardinal Wolsey, Bishop Kennion, Henry VII (during whose reign the church was built) and Edward VII (in whose reign the new doors were set in place). On the blue ribbon that twines across the door is the inscription 'The door of life is death, and life a long returning' this is a curiosity in itself as, despite extensive enquiries, no one knows its author. The ravages of time and weather took their toll and in the early 1980s the churchwardens set out to find someone to restore the paint to its original glory. They discovered in Street, Andrew Goldsworthy, who is a public house sign painter. After seeing a recent example of his work at Shepton Mallet, the wardens commissioned Mr Goldsworthy to repaint their church doors, and the result is well worth visiting. While you are in the churchyard, take note of the dovecote at the southwest corner; it is in excellent condition and is an example of the round styled dovecotes that were built in the 15th and early 16th centuries.

Places of interest in the Neighbourhood
4. The Two Little Brothers Who Never Were Parted (Petherton)
44. Where A Saxon George Fights His Dragon (Stoke-sub-Hamdon)
53. The Head Under The Seat (And The Dial Over The Porch) (Middle Chinnock)

Food and Accommodation
Both available locally

51 The Carpet On Which Once Stood A Throne

Position: St Martin of Tours Church, West Coker
Ordnance Map: Dorchester, Weymouth & surrounding area; Sheet 194
1:50 000
Map Ref: ST 5175/1470
Access: Turn north off the A30 beside the traffic lights at the Crewkerne
end of the village. The street is marked as No Through Road, and there is
parking near the entry to the church.

Note: At the time of the Coronation in 1953, a carpet was specially
woven for the site of the enthronement in Westminster Abbey.
Afterwards the carpet was cut into four sections for sale. So many
churches wished to buy a piece that lots were drawn and West Coker was
one of the winners (a second piece went to Ontario, Canada). It is still in
excellent condition despite the years that have elapsed since 1953.

The church is also worth visiting for the delightful and unusual
reredos; it was added to the altar in 1930 at the expense of Rev L. R.
Cotter, rector from 1902 until 1927, and his wife. It depicts nine figures
who represent the body of the Church and includes a bishop, a priest and
St Martin himself in the garb of a soldier.

Places of interest in the Neighbourhood
7. Tom Coryate's Much Travelled Shoes (Odcombe)
53. The Head Under The Seat (And The Dial Over The Porch) (Middle
 Chinnock)
76. The Carving By A Hero's Window (West Coker)

Food and Accommodation
Both available in West Coker; also in Yeovil and in Crewkerne

52　The Oldest Dovecote In England?

Position: Blackford
Ordnance Map: Minehead and Brendon Hills; Sheet 181 1:50 000
Map Ref: SS 9245/4535
Access: Approximately halfway along the A39 between Porlock and Minehead, take the road south to Blackford, which could easily be missed as it is just a collection of farm buildings

Note: The dovecote at Blackford, Norman in origin, dates from the 11th century and is believed to be the oldest of its kind in England. The stone walls are 4ft thick and incorporate 300 nesting holes for pigeons. The Normans introduced dovecotes following the Conquest; the design then was circular and entry for the birds was through a hole in the roof (the Blackford structure has glass over the roof entrance to keep the place dry inside because now it is used as a farm store). Later designs included square and octagonal shapes to the buildings, and the roof entry incorporated cupolas or lanterns.

Dovecotes were a means of ensuring fresh meat for the owner (always a person of means) during the winter months; farmers hated them because it was from their crops that the pigeons fed, and yet it was an offence for the birds to be killed by other than the owner or his agent. Theft of pigeons was considered so serious an offence that on the third time of conviction the thief could face death by hanging. By the same token, during the Middle Ages, pigeon keeping was severely regulated and only those in favour with the law makers were allowed to keep the birds.

Places of interest in the Neighbourhood
25.　The Gift Of A Swedish MP (Minehead)
31.　The Stone Beehive (Allerford)
42.　The Houses Protected By A Curse (Minehead)

Food and Accommodation
Both available in Minehead

53 The Head Under The Seat (And The Dial Over The Porch)

Position: St Margaret's Church, Middle Chinnock
Ordnance Map: Taunton and Lyme Regis; Sheet 193 1:50 000
Map Ref: ST 4720/1320

Note: Under a stone seat in the porch of the church the head of a cleric peers up at those entering the building. It is believed that it portrays a rector of the church at some time in the 14th century. The stone carving is very worn, but you can just make out the fact that the priest was clothed in a cope and cap. The canopy over his head (under the seat) is thought to have represented a sedilia – the seat in the sanctuary of a church for the use of the officiating priest.

As you go into the porch, look up at the strangely shaped stone above the arch. It is a sundial of a type that may well be unique. It requires no gnomon (pillar or rod) to indicate the time, but relies on the curve of the stone to cast a shadow on the side facing east that contains the hour marks.

Places of interest in the Neighbourhood
  7. Tom Coryate's Much Travelled Shoes (Odcombe)
 46. Three Manors For Three Daughters (Preston Plucknett)
 51. The Carpet On Which Once Stood A Throne (West Coker)
 76. The Carving By A Hero's Widow (West Coker)

Food and Accommodation
Available in Crewkerne and in Yeovil

54 The Inn That Was Also A Tollhouse

Position: The White Horse, Hungerford
Ordnance Map: Minehead and Brendon Hills; Sheet 181 1:50 000
Map Ref: ST 0475/4025
Access: Turn south of the A39 in Washford and, just past the ruins of
Cleeve Abbey, you will see the White Horse Inn at the junction of two
forks in the road.

Note: Records show that by 1730 this stone building was a posting inn
(the stables are still there), and a changeover point for horses on the
Barnstaple – Taunton route. The mounting block (now painted black) is
at one end of the building.

In the 18th century the government set up Turnpike Trusts to cover the
whole of England. These trusts were intended to maintain the roads in
good repair, and they were empowered to levy tolls on road users (the
1745 uprising of the Young Pretender in Scotland had convinced the
government of the day of the need for good roads when its army had got
bogged down). Unfortunately the legislators forgot to include a law

requiring the trusts to keep the roads in repair, but the tolls were avidly collected and The White Horse Inn was one of the collecting points for the Minehead United Trust from 1765 until 1877. A window was cut into the wall at the end of the building nearest to Cleeve Abbey for the purpose. The abolition of the trusts in the 19th century led to the window being blocked up on the outside, but if you decide to sample some of the food (and drink), you can see the cavity inside and the landlord will also show you where at one time a ladder passed beside the window to the bedchamber above.

Places of interest in the Neighbourhood
18. The Village Where Time Seems To Stand Still (East Quantoxhead)
25. The Gift Of A Swedish MP (Minehead)
42. The Houses Protected By A Curse (Minehead)
63. The Hunted Weathercock (Bicknoller)
73. The Village That Gave GBS A Name (Stogumber)

Food and Accommodation
Food available at The White Horse Inn; accommodation available at Minehead

55 The Church That Became A War Memorial

Position: Burrow Mump
Ordnance Map: Weston-super-Mare & Bridgwater; Sheet 182 1:50 000
Map Ref: ST 3595/3055

Note: There has been a church on the hill known as Burrow Mump since the 15th century. St Michael's Borough is a natural hill, but the top has been scarped by man, giving rise to speculation that it was a large manmade barrow. King Alfred is also associated with the Mump (he may have used it as an observation post while warring with the Danes). About 1480 a church was built on the hill; it was mentioned in contemporary writing in 1633, but twelve years later it was in ruins, and there Royalists sheltered during the Civil War. At one time there were two bells in Lyng Church, bearing the dates 1607 and 1625, that were recorded as having come from Burrow Mump. The present building dates from 1793 – William Pitt the Younger was among the subscribers; it isn't a ruin, it was just never completed. In 1946 the owner, Major A. G. Barrett, gave the hill and the church to The National Trust as a memorial to those Somerset men and women who died in the 1939-1945 war.

Places of interest in the Neighbourhood
38. The Cast-Iron Milepost (Greinton)
68. Was This Where Alfred Burnt Those Cakes? (Athelney)

Food and Accommodation
Food available at Burrowbridge; food and accommodation available in Taunton

56 Road Taxes Of The Past

Position: South Cheriton
Ordnance Map: Yeovil to Frome; Sheet 183 1:50 000
Map Ref: ST 6925/2480
Access: At the Toll House, on the southwest side of the A357

Note: During the days of the Turnpike Acts, users of main thoroughfares
paid as they went. The original tollboard is still in place on the wall of
the tollhouse at South Cheriton; as with rates today, charges varied with
the trusts (and according to the distance between tollgates). The roads in
this part of Somerset were administered by the Vale of Blackmoor Trust,
set up in 1765 and abolished in 1882.

Places of interest in the Neighbourhood
  3. The Man Who Built His Own Monument (Wincanton)
  5. The Gaol Built With Funds Filched From The Poor (Castle Cary)
 43. The Panel That Toppled A Religious Order (Templecombe)

Food and Accommodation
Both available in Wincanton

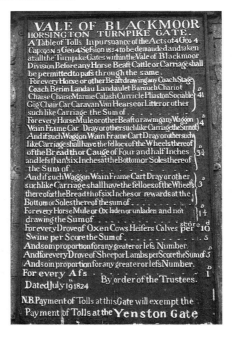

57 Fifteenth Century Market Stalls

Position: Shepton Mallet
Ordnance Map: Yeovil to Frome; Sheet 183 1:50 000
Map Ref: ST 6195/4360
Access: Make for the Market Cross in the centre of Shepton Mallet and the Shambles is in the middle of the paved square in front of the Centre (a complex containing a theatre and restaurant and other facilities which was given to the town by Francis Showering, the Babycham manufacturer).

Note: Shepton Mallet's market stall, known as a shambles (from the Latin scamellum = little bench), is believed to be the last of its kind in England. From c. 1450 onward, the north and south sides of the Market Place were lined with these stalls, which at that time were the sole preserve of butchers. During the 15th and 16th centuries, almost all market towns had similar roofed stalls. A 1912 photograph of the north side of Shepton Mallet's Market Place shows the line of shambles to be in a parlous state. In 1919 a small section was reconstructed and set up on the east side of the Market Place, and the remainder were cleared away.

The Market Cross was erected in 1500 by Walter and Agnes Buckland with a request for passers-by to pray daily for their souls.

Places of interest in the Neighbourhood
27. The Strange Building (Doulting)
61. The Stream That Powered Thirty Mills (Shepton Mallet and
    Doulting)
69. The Grave Shown On The Map (East Compton)

Food and Accommodation
Both available at Shepton Mallet

58 The Stained Glass Found In A Ditch

Position: Chewton Mendip, St Mary Magdalene Church
Ordnance Map: Weston-super-Mare & Bridgwater; Sheet 182 1:50 000
Map Ref: ST 6000/5320
Access: The church is situated at the end of a *cul-de-sac* north of the A39
at the Wells end of the village

Note: The history of the north window in the chancel of the church will
never be fully known. In 1946, Dr C. Woodforde wrote in his book,
Stained Glass in Somerset, of the window being a jumble of colours and
shapes. Today, thanks to the expert work of Jasper Kettlewell, the
window has been sorted into several disparate designs. The sections are
of several periods, beginning with the 13th century. According to the
church guide, one design, that of the Virgin weeping, was found in a
ditch outside Glastonbury by a scrap-merchant. The design was in pieces
(rather like a jigsaw puzzle before it is assembled) and the vicar, the Rev
Paul Bush, bought the scraps and incorporated them into a window in his
summerhouse. Eventually the summerhouse was pulled down. The
Church Commissioners sold the old vicarage in 1956 and the new
owners began to renovate the garden. They found a quantity of pieces of
coloured glass on the site of a piggery not far from where the
summerhouse had been. Because the pieces proved to be so attractive
when they had been washed, the owners showed the glass to Dr
Woodforde, the Dean of Wells. The dean identified most of it as being
made in the 19th century, but some fragments he placed as being of 13th-
and 14th-century origin. Mr Kettlewell was given the pieces from the
piggery as well as those that made up the existing window and eventually
Dr Woodforde's 'jumble of colours and shapes' was rearranged into the
window that you see today.

Places of interest in the Neighbourhood
12. The Italian Monument In An English Field (West Horrington)
19. The Ceiling They Didn't Know Was There (Wells)
20. The Waxworks That Thrilled The Georgians (Wookey Hole)

Food and Accommodation
Food available at Chewton Mendip; accommodation at Wells

59 The Dovecote With A Revolving Ladder

Position: Old Rectory Grounds, Dunster
Ordnance Map: Minehead and Brendon Hills; Sheet 181 1:50 000
Map Ref: SS 9910/4370
Access: Park near the Yarn Market if you can, or in the National Trust grounds of Dunster Castle – the streets of Dunster are very narrow and parking is not permitted near the church, which is on the hillside opposite the castle; nearby is the site of the old rectory.

Note: The dovecote contains a 400-year-old wooden revolving ladder (a potence) that would be remarkable today for the ingenuity of its design and execution. The ladder, which moves at the touch of a finger, was installed to allow access to each of the 500 nest boxes within the circular stone dovecote (20ft high); it consists of a central wooden post with two projecting arms at the top and the bottom to which the ladder is attached. X-ray examination showed that the post turns on a pin fixed in a beam across the floor. The pin penetrates into the post for about 7in, and on its head revolves a metal cone, probably made of bronze – which is why there is no need to oil the mechanism.

Places of interest in the Neighbourhood
25. The Gift Of A Swedish MP (Minehead)
42. The Houses Protected By A Curse (Minehead)
54. The Inn That was Also A Tollhouse (Hungerford)

Food and Accommodation
Both available in Dunster

60 The Rare Lily Crucifix

Position: Church of St John The Baptist, Wellington
Ordnance Map: Taunton and Lyme Regis; Sheet 193 1:50 000
Map Ref: ST 1405/2095

Note: The lily crucifix is to be found in the centre mullion of the east
window in the South Aisle of the church. According to one authority,
eleven other churches in England, and none in any other country, are
known to have a carving similar to this one; another authority states that
this is the only church in England known to have a lily crucifix but there
are a few also in France. Be that as it may, the lily crucifix is rare. It is
also difficult to see, which is why it escaped the destruction wrought by
Puritans upon the two niches on each side of the outer mullions; these
niches once contained figures of saints. The crucifix itself depicts a cross
budding into lilies, symbolising life in death, and traditionally was
associated with the Annunciation. The window originally stood above
the altar in the main body of the church. At one time the church was
dedicated to the Virgin Mary; there is no mention of John The Baptist
being the patron saint until 1742.

   While you are in the church, look at the tomb on the north side of the
chancel – it contains the first known epitaph in English (formerly all
were written in Latin) and commemorates a priest, Richard of
Wellington, who lived during the 14th century. The lettering is very
worn, but it reads in part … (Here?) Liggith:in:grave:IHV:CHRIST:
GODES:Sone:Grawnte:Him: (Rest?)

Places of interest in the Neighbourhood
70. The Grand Canal That Wasn't So
Grand (Nynehead)
71. The Changing Bells (Wellington)
79. Wellington's Monument (Wellington)

Food and Accommodation
Available in Wellington, but if accommodation
is fully booked, Taunton
is only a few miles along the A38

94

61 The Stream That Powered Thirty Mills

Position: Shepton Mallet and Doulting
Ordnance Map: Yeovil to Frome; Sheet 183 1:50 000
Map Ref: ST 6180/4380 and ST 6450/4324
Access: In Shepton Mallet look for the river on the north side of the town. At Doulting, park near the church and follow the signs for St Aldhelm's Well.

Note: For some 400 years the growth and prosperity of Shepton Mallet depended upon the wool trade, and the wool trade depended for its growth upon a little stream that came out of rock at Doulting and wound its way down the valley to Shepton Mallet. Although it never becomes very wide, the stream was able to power some 30 mills, many of them in quite close proximity, because of the steepness of the gradient down which it rushed. Most of these factories are gone today, but if you make for Leg Square, near the Gaol, you will see where on the east slope was a corn mill, on the north side were three factories, with a fourth in front of Barren Down House, and where a fifth factory still remains, all these powered at one time by the little River Sheppey (named, by the way for convenience, by the Ordnance Survey). Not far from Leg Square is Lower Lane, which looks much the same today as it did during the 16th and 17th centuries.

The wool trade collapsed in this area with the introduction of machinery to spin the wool and of other machines to produce cloth at a faster rate. Because they feared for their jobs, workers in the town threatened to smash new machines if they were introduced. As it was, the employers took heed, and the industry in Shepton Mallet, unable to compete with those areas that had adopted the new techniques, gradually died away.

Only a few miles east of Shepton Mallet is Doulting where the Sheppey, known in this section for many years as the River Doulting, rises. The water at the source is said to have had healing powers and for many years pilgrims to St Aldhelm's Church are believed to have bathed in the stone-lined trough in front of the arches.

Places of interest in the Neighbourhood
27. The Strange Building (Doulting)
57. Fifteenth Century Market Stalls (Shepton Mallet)
69. The Grave Shown On The Map (East Compton)

62 Willett Tower

Position: Elworthy
Ordnance Map: Minehead and Brendon Hills; Sheet 181 1:50 000
Map Ref: ST 0955/3355
Access: From the B3188 just south of Elworthy village, follow the
Handy Cross, Combe Florey road until you see the Forestry Commission
entrance to Willett Hill. Park and follow the track to the top of the hill.

Note: This folly was erected by subscription of a number of people about
the year 1774. It cost £130, Mr Bernard, Lord of the Manor of
Crowcombe contributing the bulk of the subscription with an outlay of
£80. The building is meant to represent the ruin of a Gothic gatehouse
and is 80ft high.

Places of interest in the Neighbourhood
34. The Dog Pound (And Why it was Built) (Holford)
54. The Inn That Was Also A Tollhouse (Hungerford)
73. The Village That Gave Shaw A Name (Stogumber)

Food and Accommodation
Available at Williton and Wiveliscombe

63 The Hunted Weathercock

Position: Bicknoller
Ordnance Map: Minehead and Brendon Hills; Sheet 181 1:50 000
Map Ref: ST 1110/3945
Access: Go to St George's Church at Bicknoller off the A358 (both access roads from the main road lead eventually to the church)

Note: The weathercock on the church tower has a number of holes in it. Shooting at the vane began with the Bickham family, seven of whose members died within a decade or so at the end of the 19th century, and none of whom lived to enjoy a ripe old age because of their heavy drinking. There are reports that frequently members of the family were so intoxicated at night they slept where they fell. The Bickhams were enthusiastic greyhound coursers and were famous for the champagne breakfasts they organised for the many friends who joined them for a day's coursing. If the wind was unfavourable for hunting, they would shoot at the weathercock to make it swing to the right direction. Shooting at the cock is also attributed to another well known son of Bicknoller, Harold Gimblett. Gimblett is the only first class cricketer to score a century in his debut match; he had attended a trial for a place in the Somerset team and had failed to gain a place, but as he was leaving the grounds, a message came through that one of the team would be unable to play in the match against Essex the next day. Gimblett was offered a place just for that day, made a century, and remained a Somerset player, later playing for England.

After looking around the churchyard, go into the church and see the medieval stone altar that probably was thrown out when the Mass was outlawed during the reign of Edward VI. Most of such altars were used as tomb tops, but this particular one escaped and lay in a corner of the churchyard until the 1950s when one of the churchwardens, Mr E. A. Greswell was scything the long grass and discovered it; happily this one was still complete and so could be restored and replaced.

Places of interest in the Neighbourhood
10. Where Somerset Was Going To Rival Texas (Kilve)
18. The Village Where Time Seems To Stand Still (East Quantoxhead)
54. The Inn That Was Also A Tollhouse (Hungerford)
73. The Village That Gave GBS A Name (Stogumber)

Food and Accommodation
Food available at Bicknoller and Williton; accommodation at Dunster

64 The Four Follies Of Barwick

Position: Barwick Park, near Yeovil
Ordnance Map: Dorchester, Weymouth & surrounding area; Sheet 194
1:50 000
Map Ref: ST 5595/1295; 5555/1430; 5630/1425; 5610/1485
Access: The park is privately owned and is not open to the public;
however, two of the follies can be seen easily from public highways (one
is beside the A37) and the Treacle Eater can be seen from a right of way
road that bisects the park.

Note: Little is known of the origin of all four follies in Barwick Park.
Two appear in a painting dated 1780, but there is no record of when they
were built; the others are said to have been built in order to relieve the
severe unemployment of the 1820s. The four are on the boundaries of
the park at the points of the compass with reference to the house. To the
west is a tall slender cone 75ft high. It stands on a hollow drum with
three arches and is mainly of rough stone with a smooth section topped
by a ball. To the south is an obelisk bent at the top; the 'Fish Tower' to
the north is an untapered column, 50ft high, mounted on a squared base

of random stone rubble. It is so named because at one time the capped cylindrical top was surmounted by a weather vane in the shape of a fish. There is a door on the north side of the base and the footholds inside are lighted by slits in the tower. According to local tradition, this tower was built by the Romans.

The Treacle Eater on the eastern boundary is the best known (and most ornate) of the follies of Barwick. It consists of an arch, surmounted by a central tower on top of which is a figure of Hermes. This is said to represent Jack, a runner who used to take messages to London for the Messiter family. He trained on treacle and was quite renowned for his athletic prowess during the 1770s.

Places of interest in the Neighbourhead
  7. Tom Coryate's Much Travelled Shoes (Odcombe)
16. The Brass That Became A Soap Advert (Crewkerne)
46. Three Manors For Three Daughters (Preston Plucknett)
66. The Sign Made By The Metalwork Class (Milborne Port)

Food and Accommodation
Available in Yeovil

65 When Langport Had Trains (And Floods)

Position: Bow Street Emporium
Ordnance Map: Taunton and Lyme Regis; Sheet 193 1:50 000
Map Ref: ST 4205/2675
Access: Park in the main car-park (it's free) and walk along Bow Street to the Emporium; go through to The Bistro Cafe at the back.

Note: The owner of the Bow Street Emporium has a splendid collection of photographs of Langport at the turn of the century when there were two railway stations (now there are none) and when the lower end of the town was flooded almost every spring. One photo shows a locomotive steaming along the flooded rails, another shows vessels anchored in the river offloading cargo. The photos are displayed around the walls of The Bistro Cafe so that, unlike most eateries, time spent waiting for a meal to be served passes all too quickly.

Places of interest in the Neighbourhood
17. The Tower Built By A Prime Minister (Burton Pynsent)
41. The Chapel Above The Road (Langport)
45. The Barrel Organ And The Buxom Angels (Muchelney)

Food and Accommodation
Food available at The Bistro Cafe and other establishments; accommodation somewhat limited in Langport, but if fully booked, Taunton and Bridgwater are not far away.

66 The Sign Made By The Metalwork Class

Position: Milborne Port
Ordnance Map: Yeovil to Frome; Sheet 183 1:50 000
Map Ref: ST 6835/1845
Access: On the north side of the A30, opposite Ven House

Note: About ten years ago the metalwork master of King Arthur's Secondary School in Wincanton contacted the chairman of Milborne Port Parish Council to see whether there was anything his students could do for the town. The very attractive and unusual sign on the A30 was the result. The design incorporates the local church and a waterwheel. The church is of special interest because it has in its grounds one of this country's few surviving charnel-houses (in which dead bodies and human bones are piled). Beside the entrance to the churchyard is another curiosity rarely seen today – a ball court, built in 1847 by Sir W. C. Medlycott in the earnest hope that 'this court, which is meant for the health and amusement of the town, will be protected from injury'. No one plays ball there today; it is a garden of remembrance for the dead of both World Wars.

Milborne Port was first named in a charter of AD880. From 997 to 1007 a mint in the town produced coins, some of which survive today in museums in Scandinavia – much of the money made in the smaller mints was made over to the Vikings as Danegeld, the bribe paid by weaker kings to keep marauders from our shores.

Places of interest in the Neighbourhood
 3. The Man Who Built His Own Monument (Wincanton)
43. The Panel That Toppled A Religious Order (Templecombe)

Food and Accommodation
Food available at Milborne Port; accommodation at Sherborne

67 Where's Chilly Green?

Position: Oake
Ordnance Map: Taunton and Lyme Regis; Sheet 193 1:50 000
Map Ref: ST 1750/2540
Access: From the A361 drive through Oake and take the second turning left past the Old Rectory. Take the left fork and at the second fork keep right for a few yards; the box is on the left just beyond the cottages.

Note: The Post Office obviously knows something that the Ordnance Survey department doesn't, one of its wallboxes is clearly labelled Chilly Green, and yet the only cottages within any distance of it are called Whipprells and nowhere on the map is there mention of Chilly Green. The box, made by Messrs W. T. Allen of London to a 1935 pattern, bears the cipher of George VI. It is one of the postal oddities noted by the local Letter Box Study Group. This group has a national and international membership, and meetings are held to report on discoveries of boxes of particular interest (many members have in their homes

The Chilly Green letter box.   Letter box at Higher Clavelshay Farm, Broomfield.

restored boxes that have been declared obsolete by bureaucrats or have been vandalised). If you should come across any old letter boxes that look unusual and are in out-of-the-way places, please note where they are and then phone Mrs Rosemary Berry of the Letter Box Study Group (Taunton 283649) who is trying to build up a file of those in the county.

Somerset has its share of rare letter boxes. One, at Higher Clavelshay Farm, on the Clavelshay road out of Broomfield, is the last of its type known to exist in this county. It is a lamp-box (so-called because they were usually attached to lamp poles), dating from the reign of Edward VII, and is set into the farmyard wall. Another, made by Smith & Hawkes of Birmingham, is set in the wall at Lower Ruggin Farm, not far from West Buckland. It has a hood and pediment to divert water, and because the pattern was in production only during 1859, few were made and very few (about seven) survive. The oldest known box in Somerset is not far from West Buckland at Stawley, tucked into a curved wall on the left side of the road that leads down the hill from Stawley Church. That box was also made by Messrs Smith & Hawkes (1857-1859) and has a swinging aperture to prevent rain getting in, which leads people occasionally to think the box is closed and no longer in use. The Post Office later ordered that a hood should be bolted over the aperture of such boxes to give added protection. At Cranmore, on the platform of the East Somerset Railway, is a survivor of 1929 when there was an effort to combine the Post Office and Telephone services by incorporating a letter box into a telephone kiosk.

Mrs Berry tells me that there is no such colour, officially, as pillar box red, when it is the turn of the boxes to be painted, the painter goes to the local shop and buys the cheapest available bright red paint.

Places of interest in the Neighbourhood
49. The Strange Inscription (Stawley)
60. The Rare Lily Crucifix (Wellington)
71. The Changing Bells (Wellington)
79. Wellington's Monument (Wellington)

Food and Accommodation
In Wellington, but if accommodation is unavailable, Taunton with its hotels is about ten miles away.

68 Was This Where Alfred Burnt Those Cakes?

Position: Alfred's Monument, Athelney Hill
Ordnance Map: Taunton and Lyme Regis; Sheet 193 1:50 000
Map Ref: ST 3465/2935
Access: The monument can be seen from the A361 on a low hill on the south side of the road in the section between East Lyng and Burrowbridge. For a closer look, take the road that goes obliquely east out of East Lyng (signposted to Athelney) and at Athelney Farm on the left, there is a board marked Alfred Monument; follow the road into the farmyard and the monument is in a field above the yard.

Note: All kinds of far more impressive columns commemorate far less important periods and people in England's history – but that's how it goes. John Slade of Maunsel House, owner of Athelney Farm, erected

the squat obelisk with its iron railing surround in 1801 in honour of Alfred, who became King of Wessex in 871. Alfred refused to give way to the Danes who came marauding to the West Country, and engaged them in battle several times. In 876 and 877 he freed Wareham and Exeter from the Danes, but early the following year he was surprised at his palace at Chippenham and sought refuge on the Island of Athelney. In those days, the land was undrained and the island could be reached only by boats manoeuvred by those who knew the ways through the swampy marshland. Alfred didn't stay long at Athelney, he gathered an army and at Easter, 878, he defeated the Danes at Edington (Wilts); peace was made at Wedmore and the leader of the marauders was baptised a Christian at Aller. Other gangs of Danes continued to raid England for the next six years, but eventually Alfred and his men defeated them in a mighty battle at Exeter. Alfred had two forts in this area; one at Athelney and another, connected by a bridge to the island, at Lyng. Once the immediate danger was past, Alfred built a monastery on the island, and recent excavations have shown that the east end of the church lay not far from the site of the present monument.

Places of interest in the Neighbourhood
36. Site Of The Last Battle In England (Westonzoyland)
38. The Cast-Iron Milepost (Greinton)
55. The Church That Became A War Memorial (Burrow Mump)

Food and Accommodation
Food available at Burrowbridge; food and accommodation available in Taunton

69 The Grave Shown On The Map

Position: Cannard's Grave, East Compton
Ordnance Map: Yeovil to Frome; Sheet 183 1:50 000
Map Ref: ST 6280/4175
Access: At the junction of the A371 bypass and Shepton Mallet roads

Note: Opinions differ as to whether Cannard was a king's uncle, a greedy suicide, or a felon. Correspondence in the local press at the beginning of this century identified Cannard with Kenred, a wealthy pagan, uncle to King Ina, who died about the beginning of the 8th century. Ina had converted to Christianity and was buried in sanctified ground upon his death, but uncle Kenred may have been buried where Cannard's Grave Inn now stands.

Another theory concerning the grave's occupant deals with one, Giles Cannard, an innkeeper of the mid-17th century. He was prospering, but he wanted more money and to obtain it he committed forgery. Cannard was found out, disgrace followed and he hanged himself. In accordance with the custom of the day, he was buried where the two roads meet near the site of his inn.

Finally, there is the theory that Cannard was a felon who committed a crime so dastardly that even today it mustn't be talked about openly – one of those stories to be told within the confines of the home when the children are old enough to know – and he was buried where those who tried him hanged him.

Places of interest in the Neighbourhood
27. The Strange Building (Doulting)
57. Fifteenth Century Market Stalls (Shepton Mallet)
61. The Stream That Powered Thirty Mills (Shepton Mallet and Doulting)

Food and Accommodation
Cannard's Grave Inn offers food and the inn at Doulting offers both food and accommodation; there are also hotels in Shepton Mallet.

70 The Grand Canal That Wasn't So Grand

Position: Nynehead
Ordnance Map: Minehead and Brendon Hills; Sheet 181 1:50 000
Map Ref: ST 1350/2285
Access: Take the A38 as far as the roundabout on the Taunton side of
Wellington, follow the signs for Wellington until you reach the road to
the right with signs indicating Poole Tip, Nynehead. Take that road and
after driving under a railway bridge you will see Wharf Cottage on the
right. Stop and park. Opposite the cottage is a gate and a stile leading to a
footpath through a copse. The path follows the course of the iron
aqueduct that carried the Grand Canal over the private drive to Nynehead
Court. Not far away are the remains of a lift.

Note: The Grand Western Canal was authorised by an Act of Parliament
in 1796. It was to run from the tideway of the Exe near Topsham and
extend to the River Tone at Taunton, with branches from Burlescombe
to Tiverton, another at Cullompton and a third at Wellington. This,
being before the advent of the railway, was intended to open up the West
Country for the easy and cheap transportation of coal, lime and
limestone. By the time work began in 1810, the original concept had
shrunk and Tiverton was the end of the line instead of Topsham. The
estimate of the cost for the entire network was £220,000; when the
Tiverton to Holcombe Rogus branch (the first completed section)
opened on August 25 1814 (11 miles of waterway without a single lock),
more than that amount had already been spent. The whole length of the
canal was eventually operational in 1838, and it never did show a profit
for its shareholders. One problem was that between Taunton and
Greenham the canal had a rise of 262ft; the engineer, James Green,
either had to construct many series of locks (which were expensive in
construction and in terms of time taken to negotiate them) or he had to
devise another means of raising and lowering vessels over the terrain.
He decided to construct one inclined plane of 81ft (near Wellisford) and
designed seven lifts, the highest of which (near Trefusis Farm, Bradford-
on-Tone) raised vessels 38ft to pass over the River Tone. The lift on the
south side of the Tone at Nynehead Court Lodge was 24ft high.

By 1867 the railway had come to Somerset, and the first closure took
place. The first branch opened was the last to close (1924), and today all
that remains are a few short stretches of water courses and a few ruined
buildings. The Nynehead iron aqueduct has probably remained in the

The stone arch built to carry the Grand Western Canal over the driveway to Nynehead Court – itself now overgrown.

best condition, the lift nearby has lost all its machinery but is thought to be the most complete of the seven, but also, not far from the Victory Inn near Allerford are some more buildings, relics of the Grand Western Canal.

Places of interest in the Neighbourhood
 1. One Of The Gems Of The Great Exhibition (Taunton)
48. The Tower That's Made Of Leather (Taunton)
60. The Rare Lily Crucifix (Wellington)
67. Where's Chilly Green? (Oake)
71. The Changing Bells (Wellington)
72. Where Lepers Once Were Tended (Taunton)
78. The Toads That Children Love (Taunton)

Food and Accommodation
Both available at Taunton

110

71 The Changing Bells

Position: Eight Bells Inn, Wellington
Ordnance Map: Taunton and Lyme Regis; Sheet 193 1:50 000
Map Ref: ST 1415/2075
Access: On the High Street near to the Church of St John the Baptist

Note: Although the Eight Bells is not Wellington's oldest inn (the Three
Cups predates the Monmouth Rebellion), it has an interesting history. It
stands on land that until the beginning of this century was owned by the
church, and so presumably began as a hostelry associated with the
church. Records of 1728 show that the inn (then known as the Five Bells
because the church had a peal of five) was rated at £1 per annum. As
other Wellington hostelries were rated as high as £5 a year, it would
seem that the Five Bells did not attract a very wealthy clientele. The
name changed to the Eight Bells in 1748 when Richard Bovett presented
three new bells to the church on the occasion of his marriage. Recently
discovered victuallers' licensing records date to 1755. At first the
landlord's name was not given; then, in 1766, some bright lad hit on the
idea of noting the licensee's name against that of the inn, and the Eight
Bells is recorded as having Simon Shuttock as landlord until 1775. Then
both names disappeared and James Nowland is shown as licensee of The
Ring of Bells for 1777; whether it was an effort by the landlord to change
the name of the inn, or a bureaucratic error, will probably never be
known, but the next year's entry sees the resurgence of the Eight Bells
with James Nowland as the landlord, and thus the inn has been known
ever since.

Places of interest in the Neighbourhood
67. Where's Chilly Green? (Oake)
70. The Grand Canal That Wasn't So Grand (Nynehead)
79. Wellington's Monument (Wellington)

Food and Accommodation
Good food available at the Eight Bells; some accommodation in the
town, but ample available in Taunton.

72 Where Lepers Once Were Tended

Position: Lisieux Way, Taunton
Ordnance Map: Taunton and Lyme Regis; Sheet 193 1:50 000
Map Ref: ST 2390/2475
Access: From the centre of Taunton, follow the signs for the A358 but turn right at the traffic lights at the far end of East Reach (past the old East Reach Hospital, now closed) and immediately swing left. The one-time leper hospital is the long low thatched building with a Community Council sign (rather like an inn sign) outside.

Note: This building was at one time a lazar or spytel house for the care of those with 'loathesome' diseases, especially lepers. It was founded in 1185 as the Hospital of the Holy Ghost and St Margaret; documents of 1180 pertaining to the Augustinian Priory of Taunton refer to the chapel of St Margaret 'infirmorum', and as these documents show that there was also a cemetery and land for the use of the inmates, it seems that the hospital replaced one existing before 1174 which stood outside the East Gate of the town. All men shunned lepers who, if they went into towns or villages, were obliged by law to carry a bell to warn people of their approach. Abbot Richard Beere of Glastonbury rebuilt St Margaret's some time between 1510 and 1515 (there is a local legend that the building had been destroyed by fire, but documentary confirmation has yet to come to light). By 1547 the scourge of leprosy had lessened and St Margaret's had been converted to 13 almshouses for the accommodation of 26 persons. Under the same roof was the chapel, which was sold off in 1549 to John Norres by the power of the Act for the Suppression of Hospitals, Chapels and Chantries. Fortunately, during the reign of Elizabeth another Act was passed to redress the harm done by the

wholesale grabbing of money and lands set aside for charitable purposes and, from 1612, St Margaret's Hospital was again able to enjoy the full use of its endowments. Records show that from 1750 onwards, six or seven deserving poor women, each with her own one-up, one-down dwelling, lived in the almshouses free of rent. By 1936 the almshouses were considered unfit for human habitation and were threatened with demolition. The Rural Community Council acted to save the building (new almshouses were built) and since 1939 St Margaret's has served as the offices for the Community Council for Somerset and as a Rural Crafts Centre.

Although the building is in fulltime use, it is possible to go inside and look around if you telephone Taunton 331222 to arrange a convenient time.

Places of interest in the Neighbourhood
1. One Of The Gems Of The Great Exhibition (Taunton)
48. The Tower That's Made Of Leather (Taunton)
68. Was This Where Alfred Burnt Those Cakes? (Athelney)
78. The Toads That Children Love (Taunton)

Food and Accommodation
Available in Taunton

73 The Village That Gave GBS A Name

Position: Stogumber
Ordnance Map: Minehead and Brendon Hills; Sheet 181 1:50 000
Map Ref: ST 0985/3730

Note: George Bernard Shaw, author of *Pygmalion (My Fair Lady)*, was always careful to see that the names of characters in his plays were not those of people still alive (a very canny man was GBS). In 1923 he contacted the then rector of Stogumber to discover whether the place was named after a family, and if so, whether there was anyone of that name still alive. Upon being informed that the name was a corruption either of Stoke Warner, Warver or Gomer, and that there certainly was no one of that name living so far as the rector was aware, Shaw knew that he had named another character, Bishop Stogumber, in what many scholars consider to be his finest play – *Saint Joan*.

Places of interest in the Neighbourhood
18. The Village Where Time Seems To Stand Still (East Quantoxhead)
54. The Inn That Was Also A Tollhouse (Hungerford)
62. Willett Tower (Elworthy)

Food and Accommodation
Food available in Stogumber; accommodation in Taunton or Minehead

74 The Smallest Parish Church In England

Position: St Beuno's Church, Culbone
Ordnance Map: Minehead and Brendon Hills; Sheet 181 1:50 000
Map Ref: ST 8425/4835
Access: Is only by footpath; the easiest route entails leaving the A39 opposite the inn that is west of the road fork at Oare Post and keeping to the left-hand path until you reach the Coast Path. Where the path forks at Silcombe Farm, turn right to reach the church. Approximately two miles of walking.

Note: With the closure of so many small churches, Culbone (originally called Kitnor) now holds the record for being the smallest complete parish church in England and, furthermore, services are still held there

regularly. The nave measures 12ft 4in by 21ft 6in, and the chancel is 10ft by 13ft 6in. The door and walls are 12th century in origin and the nave, roof and pews date from the 15th century. The font is said to have been carved in Sussex in 1089 and taken to Culbone in 1897 during renovations. The church can accommodate 36 worshippers, each pew is wide enough to seat two.

The dedication is somewhat doubtful (Beuno was a Celtic abbot who converted North Wales in the mid-7th century and founded a monastery of sorts at Clynnog-fawr, on the coast of Caernarfon Bay), but it is almost certain that the church is of Celtic foundation.

Places of interest in the Neighbourhood
15. The Village Where Eight Bridges Aren't Enough (Winsford)
37. The Case Of The Missing Body (Cow Castle)
80. The Steepest Motorable Hill In England (Porlock)

Food and Accommodation
Available at Porlock and Minehead

75 The Mini-Follies Of Frome

Position: 2 Mount Pleasant, Frome
Ordnance Map: Yeovil to Frome; Sheet 183 1:50 000
Map Ref: ST 7745/4965
Access: Take the Spring Gardens road out of Frome and turn beside the Farmers Arms into an unmade cul-de-sac. No 2 is about 20 yards up the hill.

Note: Follies are not the sole prequisite of the rich as Mr Hall, a Frome resident, showed some 25 years ago. Following his retirement, he collected stones from various sources and built a delightful series of mini-follies in his front garden. In those days Mount Pleasant was on the highway coming out of Frome and many people found pleasure in stopping to look at the little buildings. Today there are few visitors, but the present owner, Mr Ian Vine (who has been there for 22 years), has maintained the follies and allows those people who wish to look around his front garden.

Places of interest in the Neighbourhood
   9. The Horse In The Church (Mells)
  33. The Littlest Sunday School (Frome)
  77. The Church In The Farmyard (Hardington Bampfylde)

Food and Accommodation
Both available in Frome

76 The Carving By A Hero's Widow

Position: West Coker Manor House
Ordnance Map: Dorchester, Weymouth & surrounding area; Sheet 194
1:50 000
Map Ref: ST 5175/1360
Access: In the village of West Coker, turn into Manor Street from the
A30 and the Manor House stands on the south side

Note: West Coker House is open to the public during the month of
August ONLY; for the rest of the year it is a private residence.

There has been a manor at West Coker since pre-Conquest times; the
Domesday Commissioners noted that it was held by the king as part of
the forfeited property of Gytha, widow of Earl Godwin and mother of
Harold (killed 1066 at the Battle of Hastings). The old house was burnt
down in 1457 during a peasant uprising (led, it is believed, by the village
priest). Part of the present house dates from 1473.

In 1908, Sir Matthew Nathan, one-time Governor of Natal, of Hong
Kong and of Queensland, bought the Manor House as a retreat. He was
Second Secretary for Ireland at the time of the 1916 Easter Uprising, and
was working alone in Dublin Castle when the rebels attempted to take
over the country.

Sir Matthew commissioned Sir Aston Webb to design the southwest
wing of his beloved house as a library. The quarry on Ham Hill, which
had supplied stone for the rest of the house, was again called upon to
supply building material; and Kathleen Scott, the sculptress (who was
married first to Scott of the Antarctic and later to Baron Kennet), carved
the figure that is over the fireplace. Her most famous work is the bronze
statue of Robert Falcon Scott that stands in Waterloo Place, London.

If you are able to visit the manor, look for the 'squint', a small
opening high in the north wall of the Great Hall from which people
upstairs could see what was happening below (very useful during time of
unrest in the land, but also it came in handy when the manor housed a
school!). The windows on the staircase near the squint are said to include
15th century glass.

Places of interest in the Neighbourhood
16. The Brass That Became A Soap Advert (Crewkerne)
30. The Head Under The Seat (And The Dial Over The Porch) Middle
     Chinnock)
46. Three Manors For Three Daughters (Preston Plucknett)
51. The Carpet Where Once Stood A Throne (West Coker)

77 The Church In The Farmyard

Position: Hardington
Ordnance Map: Yeovil to Frome; Sheet 183 1:50 000
Map Ref: ST 7425/5260
Access: On the A362 between Buckland Down and Buckland Dinham, turn north when you reach a road flanked by two tall stone gateposts. Drive until you reach a sign indicating Farm to the left and Church to the right. Follow the latter road.

Note: St Mary's Church at Hardington Bampfylde is one of the many disused churches kept open by the Redundant Churches Fund. Such buildings remain consecrated and are used for occasional church services.

St Mary's was used by the Bampfylde family, local landowners. The building contains remnants of a 12th century church, and records show that during the Black Death, in 1348 and 1349, there were three rectors, so it may be assumed that two died with their parishioners. The congregation was fairly sizeable at that time, but it never recovered in numbers after the plague.

The north wall has fragments of medieval wall paintings on it, but it is almost impossible to decipher what was the subject. The church also has

a board painted with the Royal Arms of Charles I dated 1640, it is remarkable in escaping the purge that took place during the Commonwealth. Hardington has had several colourful owners. One, Sir Charles Bampfylde, succeeded to the property in 1776. He was a friend of the Prince of Wales (Prinny) and was rather dissolute throughout his life. He died in 1823 at the age of 70, shot by a man whose wife 'lived in the service of Sir Charles'. The shot didn't kill him, a piece of wire from his braces entered the wound, corroded and caused gangrene. The Rev J. R. Jolliffe of Ammerdown (see 35) performed the funeral service.

One wonders why Sir Charles's illegitimate son, the Rev, C. F. B. Bampfylde, didn't officiate as he had been appointed to the living by his father in 1814.

The churchyard is surrounded by the buildings of modern-day farming, but if worshippers of a hundred years ago were to return today, they would probably find little altered inside. The stained glass windows have been replaced by plain glass, but nine panelled box pews remain and so does the clerk's desk and pulpit (these and the squire's pew opposite date from c. 1780, the remainder are c. 1815). If you find the door locked, call at the farmhouse for the key, and then don't forget to return it.

Places of interest in the Neighbourhood
28. Nunney's Moving Cross
33. The Littlest Sunday School (Frome)
35. Rival Towers (Ammerdown Park)
75. The Mini-Follies of Frome

Food and Accommodation
Food available at Buckland Dinham; food and accommodation available at Frome

78 The Toads That Children Love

Position: Taunton
Ordnance Map: Taunton and Lyme Regis; Sheet 193 1:50 000
Map Ref: ST 2275/2445
Access: The Old Market Centre is situated between the pedestrian High
Street and Fore Street in Taunton. Look for W. H. Smith's and Marks &
Spencer's and entries to the complex are on the opposite side of the
street.

Note: Development of The Old Market Centre took place behind three
massive hoardings between 1977 and 1982. When the complex opened
on November 16, 1982, it seemed to be a case of overnight
transformation for Taunton. The architect had commissioned two young
sculptors from Wells to create a centrepiece with a water-based theme
for the open area between the shops; Philippa Threlfall and Kennedy
Collings produced three splendid toads, cast in fibreglass to resemble
bronze and studded with ceramic stones. The animals crouch beside a
ripple pond surrounded by bench seats upon which people can rest.
Young children seem to find the toads of just the right size and texture to
climb on and to touch, and the sculptures certainly are an unusual focal
point for a shopping development.

Places of interest in the Neighbourhood
  1. One Of The Gems Of The Great Exhibition (Taunton)
 48. The Tower That's Made Of Leather (Taunton)
 72. Where Lepers Once Were Tended (Taunton)

Food and Accommodation
Ample food and plenty of choice of lodgings available in Taunton

79 Wellington's Monument

Position: On the Blackdown Hills above Wellington
Ordnance Map: Taunton and Lyme Regis; Sheet 193 1:50 000
Map Ref: ST 1350/1725
Access: From the Wellington Bypass of the A38, follow the road marked Monument

Note: Following his victory over the French at Talavera in 1809, Arthur Wellesley was ennobled and had to select a title. He was overseas, so his brother William chose one for him – Wellington – a town Arthur had never been to, but which sounded very like his family name. Also the Wellesleys claimed to have gone to Ireland in the 13th century from Somerset, so there was a slight connection. Arthur bought two Wellington manors with the £100,000 voted by Parliament to him in 1813, and on September 28, 1819 he visited the town to see his estates. The monument that stands above the town must hold some kind of record for the length of time it took abuilding. William Sanford of Nynehead suggested a monument to the Duke in 1815, and by December of that year £1450 had been raised by public subscription. The winning entry in a design competition required a 95ft pillar surmounted by a cast iron figure of the duke, with three cottages incorported in the base for occupation by veteran soldier caretakers. By 1818 the column was 47ft high and the money gone. A further appeal brought the height to 121ft in 1820 but with no statue. It was struck by lightning in 1846 and not until the duke's death in 1852 was it repaired, when the column was then taken up to 170ft with a conical cap (no statue, no cottages and caretakers either). Then, with a later restoration in 1892, the column reached its present height of 175ft (still no statue).
  That's not the end of the saga. Twenty four brass cannon, captured at Waterloo, were to be placed around the base. A brass cannon and 15 iron ones were taken from Woolwich Arsenal in June 1818 and shipped to Exeter Quay, and there they stayed. Ten were sunk into the ground eventually, to act as bollards, the brass gun was sold for £64 in 1837 to defray corporation costs, and when in 1890 Exeter was approached to see whether Wellington could have four cannon, it was found they were naval cannon, cast in Scotland in 1789 and never were at Waterloo. In October 1910 the guns were at last hauled to Wellington and set in place. They stayed there until 1940 when they were removed for scrap metal, but as the demand for such metal fell, the guns were buried at Watchet.

In 1977 the last remaining cannon was brought from Exeter and eventually installed in 1984.

Places of interest in the Neighbourhood
49. The Strange Inscription (Stawley)
60. The Rare Lily Crucifix (Wellington)
71. The Changing Bells (Wellington)

Food and Accommodation
Both available at Wellington

80 The Steepest Motorable Hill In England

Position: Porlock Hill
Ordnance Map: Minehead and Brendon Hills; Sheet 181 1:50 000
Map Ref: ST 8750/4630 to 8830/4660
Access: Up from the Minehead side of the A39; down from the Lynton side of the A39. WARNING: Do not attempt to drive either up or down this hill if your vehicle is not in good repair.

Note: Ponder, as you negotiate this hill (which at times has a gradient of 1 in 4), that in January 1899, during a very severe storm, the crew of the Lynmouth lifeboat were unable to launch their craft from the harbour, so they hauled it, with the help of teams of horses and able-bodied men of the town, over Countisbury and Porlock. The journey took some thirteen hours, but, when the weary men eventually were able to launch the lifeboat from the calmer waters of Porlock Weir, they succeeded in rescuing some of the sailors they had set out to save.

Places of interest in the Neighbourhood
15. The Village Where Eight Bridges Aren't Enough (Winsford)
31. The Stone Beehive (Allerford)
74. The Smallest Parish Church In England (Culbone)

Food and Accommodation
Available at Porlock, Lynmouth and Minehead

Index